THE GREAT CANOES

S0-AGQ-168

THE GREAT CANOES

REVIVING A NORTHWEST COAST TRADITION

DAVID NEEL

Afterword by
TOM HEIDLEBAUGH

Douglas & McIntyre
Vancouver / Toronto

University of Washington Press
Seattle

Text and photographs copyright © 1995 by David Neel

Afterword copyright © 1995 by Tom Heidlebaugh

95 96 97 98 99   5 4 3 2 1

All rights reserved. No part of this book may be reproduced, stored in a retrieval system or transmitted in any form or by any means, without the prior permission of the publisher or, in Canada, in the case of photocopying or other reprographic copying, a licence from CANCOPY (Canadian Reprography Collective), Toronto, Ontario.

Douglas & McIntyre Ltd.
1615 Venables Street
Vancouver, British Columbia V5L 2H1

Canadian Cataloguing in Publication Data

Neel, David.
    The Great Canoes
    ISBN 1-55054-185-4

    1. Indians of North America — British Columbia — Boats. 2. Canoes and canoeing —
British Columbia. I. Title.
E78.B9N43 1995   387.2'9   C95-910061-X

Published simultaneously in the United States of America by
The University of Washington Press
P.O. Box 50096
Seattle, Washington 98145-5096

Library of Congress Cataloging-in-Publication Data

Neel, David.
    The great canoes /David Neel; afterword by Tom Heidlebaugh.
       p. cm.
    Includes bibliographical references.
    ISBN 0-295-97482-6 (alk. paper)

    [1. Indians of North America — Northwest, Pacific — Boats. 2. Canoes and canoeing —
Northwest, Pacific.] I. Title.
E78.N77N44 1995   623.8'29 — dc20   95-10804   CIP

Editing by Barbara Pulling
Cover and text design by Jim Skipp
Inside cover photograph: Canoe-building near Masset, B.C., 1897.
    Courtesy of the Royal British Columbia Museum, PN5409.
Map by Eric Leinberger
Typeset by NovaType Inc.
Typefaces: New Baskerville and Cochin
Printed and bound in Hong Kong by C&C Offset Printing Co. Ltd.
Printed on acid-free paper

The author wishes to acknowledge the Cultural Services Branch, British Columbia Ministry of Tourism, Small Business and Culture for their support of this book.

The publisher gratefully acknowledges the assistance of the Canada Council and of the British Columbia Ministry of Tourism, Small Business and Culture for its publishing programs.

Frontispiece photograph: *The Namgis canoe,* G̱aluda, *anchored out
for the evening at Fort Rupert, B.C.*

CONTENTS

For my precious children:
Jamie, Ellen, Edwin, Alvin and Simon

Each person I interviewed is identified by nation. In books and magazines Native peoples are often identified by linguistic group: Tsimshian, Coast Salish, etc. This practice is historically inaccurate and can be misleading. All the Kwakwala-speaking people, for example, are referred to as "Kwagiutl" or "Kwakiutl" (or most recently "Kwakwaka'wakw") even though we live over an area that extends as far south as Comox and as far north as Kitimat. We are actually approximately twenty nations, including the Namgis, the Gwa'sala'Nakwaxda'xw, the Weiwaikai, and so on. "Kwagiutl" is correct usage only for the people of Fort Rupert. Many First Nations today no longer use these linguistic groupings. For this book, each person's nation is identified as he or she sees it. Since the term "Kwakwaka'wakw" has become part of contemporary culture, I have decided to use it in my introduction, even though my elders tell me it is not accurate historically.

Current place of residence is given for each person I interviewed so that readers can get an idea of the extent of the canoe resurgence and its impact on various communities.

CANOE NATIONS OF THE NORTHWEST COAST

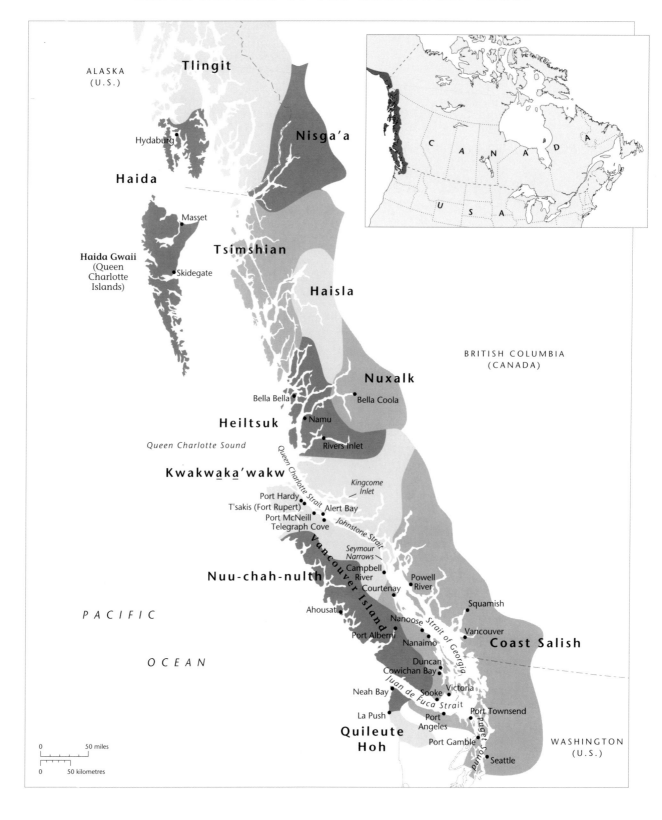

ALASKA
(U.S.)

Tlingit

Hydaburg

Nisga'a

Haida

Masset

Haida Gwaii
(Queen
Charlotte
Islands)

Skidegate

Tsimshian

Haisla

BRITISH COLUMBIA
(CANADA)

Nuxalk

Bella Bella • Bella Coola

Heiltsuk
• Namu

Queen Charlotte Sound

Rivers Inlet

Kwakw<u>a</u>k<u>a</u>'wakw

*Kingcome
Inlet*

Port Hardy
T'sakis (Fort Rupert) • Alert Bay
Port McNeill
Telegraph Cove

Johnstone Strait

*Seymour
Narrows*

Nuu-chah-nulth

Campbell
River
Courtenay

Powell
River

Squamish

Ahousat

Nanoose

Vancouver Island

Port Alberni
Nanaimo

Vancouver

Coast Salish

Strait of Georgia

PACIFIC

Duncan

Cowichan Bay

OCEAN

Neah Bay

Sooke
Victoria

Juan de Fuca Strait

Port Townsend

La Push

Port
Angeles

**Quileute
Hoh**

Port Gamble

WASHINGTON
(U.S.)

Seattle

CANADA

U S A

0   50 miles

0   50 kilometres

This book is about a journey:
the journey of many nations, the journey of
the great canoes of the First Peoples
of the Pacific Northwest.

These majestic vessels, crafted from a single log often hundreds of years old, all but disappeared early in this century. It is hard to explain why so little has been written about them, as they are probably the single most important aspect of Northwest Coast culture. To the Kwakwaka'wakw, the Haida, the Coast Salish, the Tsimshian, the Nuu-chah-nulth, the Tlingit and other coastal groups, the canoe was as important as the automobile is now to North America. With one crucial difference: the canoe was a spiritual vessel that was the object of great respect, from its life as a tree in the forest to its falling to earth as a log and finally its landing on the beach as a finished craft. As you read the words that follow, you will understand that respect continues to be a vital aspect of the contemporary canoe experience. The people speaking in these pages are some of those who make up the canoe community that has developed over the last several years. They dream big dreams, setting aside vast periods of time and sacrificing their financial security to live their culture. They have contributed to the return of the great canoe.

The canoe is today, as it has always been, much more than just a boat. The legends of the Pacific Coast First Nations tell of the time of the great flood, when the people tied their canoes together side by side. As the waters rose, the people took a stout cedar rope and attached their canoes to a mountaintop. Here they waited until the waters receded, and they were saved. Today, in its renaissance, the canoe carries the knowledge of a millennia-old culture as well as the dreams and aspirations of a younger generation. It is a vessel of knowledge, symbolizing the cultural regeneration of many nations as they struggle to retain and rebuild following a period of systematic oppression and of rapid social and technological change. The great canoe has come back from the abyss a vital symbol for First Nations. Once a mode of transport, allowing our people to fish, gather food, trade and travel, it has evolved today into a healing vessel, deeply

1

affecting all those who come into contact with it. Young people particularly benefit from learning the way of the canoe.

The canoe is a metaphor for community; in the canoe, as in any community, everyone must work together. Paddling or "pulling" as a crew over miles of water requires respect for one another and a commitment to working together, as the old people did. All facets of the contemporary canoe experience — planning, building, fund-raising, practising, travelling — combine to make our communities strong and vital in the old ways. There was a time not long ago when we lived several families to a bighouse and knew our family histories, by memory, for several generations back. We depended on one another for our livelihood. In front of our houses we constructed an *awakawis,* or meeting place, where we would pass the time, get to know our neighbours, be human together. The contemporary canoe is bringing families, villages and nations together again to work and share. First Nations who have historically been enemies, or have had long-standing issues dividing them, visit one another on our canoe journeys, hosting where once there was animosity. The canoe is helping us to be more human again. We work for something besides income; for a few precious days or weeks we forget about the clock, live by the tides. We stay up late in the villages we visit, singing and dancing, sharing our homes and our cultures. I have never before felt the level of brotherhood and sisterhood that comes out at our canoe gatherings.

The comeback of the canoe is a recent phenomenon. The magnificent fifty-foot *LooTaas* (Wave Eater), created in 1985–86, was one of the earliest of the great canoes to be built during this period of renaissance. Eminent Haida master Bill Reid, the head carver, was assisted by Guujaaw and Simon Dick as well as a number of others. Reid first carved a smaller canoe, using lines and measurements taken from a canoe in a museum collection, then adapted these measurements for the *LooTaas.* The fine vessel became an important addition to Haida culture, carrying Reid and a crew up the Seine River to Paris, France, in 1989 and travelling from Haida Gwaii to Hydaburg, Alaska, the same year to reconnect two nations divided by the imposition of the Canada/U.S. border. A mould was made from the *LooTaas,* and fibreglass replicas, visually almost indistinguishable from the original once in the water, were produced. The importance of the *LooTaas* to the Haida underlines the need for a canoe to be used as a living part of First Nations culture.

The contemporary resurgence of the canoe is marked by a series of "paddles" that have significance far beyond the mere journeys involved. The Heiltsuk people travelled in 1986 from

2

their home in Bella Bella to the world's fair in Vancouver, but it was the 1989 Paddle to Seattle journey that spawned the revival of the great canoes among the ocean-going First Nations of the Pacific Northwest. Many people were involved in the planning of this paddle, which took place during celebrations marking Washington State's 100th anniversary, but the late David Forlines, Terri Tavenner and Emmett Oliver were pivotal figures. In July of 1989 a canoe from Hoh, Washington, and two from La Push left for Golden Gardens, outside of Seattle, where they converged with a flotilla of Suquamish, Tulalip, Lummi and Heiltsuk canoes. Here a message was delivered to the people of Washington State. Signed by twenty-one Washington First Nations, it contained the words of the great Duwamish leader Chief Seattle, who had prophesied in 1855 that Native people, the traditional keepers of the land, would have to entrust the non-Native nation with that role. "The bones of your ancestors are now under your feet as ours have been for millenia," the document reads. "We ask you to become true Americans, caretakers of our good Mother Earth and the great waters flowing with, not on, this place now called Washington State. We lived and died here for hundreds of generations, and we offer our assistance in your coming to balance as an adult."

It was during this gathering at Golden Gardens that the Qatuwas Festival was born. A member of the Heiltsuk canoe, Frank Brown, issued an invitation to all the canoe nations to gather in Bella Bella in four years' time. After conferring with the others present, David Forlines accepted the invitation. Brown was given the paddle of the senior Quileute elder and told, "We will come and get it in four years." Some questioned Brown's authority to issue such an invitation and oblige the Heiltsuk people as hosts, but in the end it was largely his energy and vision that fuelled this pivotal event.

As word of the Qatuwas Festival circulated on the moccasin telegraph, enthusiasm grew. Many First Nations built canoes and started paddling for the first time in a century. The Heiltsuk rose to the occasion, hosting twenty-three canoes from up and down the coast. Qatuwas, in the Kwakwala language of the Heiltsuk Nation, means "people gathered together in one place," and close to two thousand people attended the week-long gathering in Bella Bella in the summer of 1993. It would be difficult to overstate the importance of this event. In his welcome speech, Heiltsuk Tribal Council Chairman Edwin Newman said, "Native people are regaining their strength and culture, and this gathering is a sign that things are changing for our people."

The 1994 Tribal Journeys paddle, which began in Oweekeno, B.C., brought a number of canoes to Victoria for the opening of the Commonwealth Games. Each canoe carried the Queen's Baton through its traditional territory. Chief Frank Nelson, Musgama, and Danny Henry, Coast Salish, were the driving energy behind Tribal Journeys. This paddle was not without controversy, as some felt the First Nations were being exploited by the Commonwealth countries, many of which have a history of poor treatment of their aboriginal citizens.

The next big journey in the four-year cycle will be the 1997 paddle to La Push, Washington, at the invitation of the Quileute Nation. This is expected to be the largest gathering to date. We are anticipating smaller journeys every summer until then.

The contemporary canoe has evolved into an important political tool. It serves to reinforce the existence and continuation of First Nations peoples and cultures in a social/political landscape that has endeavoured to make us invisible. What greater way to assert our presence, and the indomitability of our traditional culture, than by bringing fifteen or twenty great canoes into a coastal harbour? No one can help but be impressed by the graceful lines of these majestic ocean vessels. The Haida Nation have used their vessel, the *LooTaas,* to protest unregulated sport fishing in their traditional waters. The *LooTaas* is hard to ignore, all fifty feet of it, the prow rising six feet above the water.

The personal cost, in both income and time, can be very high for the builders and the paddlers of the great canoes. As one young paddler told me, "Our culture is expensive." A twenty-five-foot canoe costs about $30,000 to $35,000 to make. While some nations have sufficient funds to undertake the building of a large canoe, they are the exception. Many canoes are built by smaller villages, and in other cases an individual initiates the project. The paddlers too make a significant investment. The crew from Washington State travelled for two months on their epic journey to Bella Bella in 1993. Such a major commitment speaks to the value these pullers place on reviving a canoe tradition among their people. At one time, whole villages would travel by canoe to visit and feast during the winter ceremonies. Spending two months away from home was possible, and not uncommon. Today, to take a sixth of your year to practise your culture is nearly impossible. As Tom Jackson of the Quileute told me during our 1994 paddle to Victoria, "We just got our bills paid off from our trip to Bella Bella last year, and it was time to leave again." His village is now committed to hosting the 1997 gathering, so it may be 1998 before they get on top of their financial obligations again. The revival of our great canoes has been achieved through the tenacity of a relative handful of people who have put aside their personal needs to support our traditions.

Carving the canoe is a big responsibility: the carver takes the lives of future travellers in his or her hands. Traditionally, a carver followed a disciplined regime. Before he began, he would prepare himself spiritually through fasting, prayer and sweatlodge. He would abstain from sexual relations and avoid combing his hair so that cracks would not develop in the canoe. After making a test hole with elbow adze and chisel to check for inside rot, the carver would fell the ancient cedar himself using hand tools, a formidable job. A prayer was then said for the cedar, and an offering of thanks was given for its sacrifice for the canoe builder and his family. The carver did his work over a two-year period. He would rough-shape the log, first removing the bark and sapwood using an axe and an elbow adze. Then he would taper the ends and take out the wood between the high stern and bow. At this point the log would be left to "season" over the winter. This step was crucial in ensuring that the canoe did not crack too badly in later stages of carving. The following year, the carver returned with men from his village and towed the log to the ocean, where it was floated to a carving site on the beach. Here the canoe was finished.

The canoe site became a meeting place as people gathered to watch the canoe take shape. The old-timers used tools made from the incisor teeth of beavers, nephrite and jadeite. Metal from shipwrecks that washed ashore — a material later obtained through trade — was used very early on. There were many different styles of canoe on the coast, with each tribal group, each village and each canoe builder having a distinctive design. There were also many types: sealing, whaling, freight, river, fishing and, most well known, the war canoe.

The carver would establish the exterior lines of the canoe first. Next the inside would be hollowed out, with the carver using wedges to split out large sections, then controlled burning and finally adzing to complete the work. The final stage in shaping the canoe was to use hot rocks and water to steam-bend the sides outwards. Steaming also drew the bow and stern upwards as well as adding to the strength of the vessel. Following this, prow and stern pieces were added, and thwarts and seats installed. The exterior had to be surfaced, and many carvers did this by charring the wood with fire and then rubbing away the charred portion. This process would remove burrs, harden the wood and draw the natural oils to the surface to act as a protectant. Finally the canoe was given a name, and it was ready to begin its life on the water.

Spirituality is still an integral part of the canoe experience. The blessing of the log is an important prerequisite to carving a traditional canoe. We give thanks to the cedar and acknowledge the spirit of the log. A canoe, coming from a soul sometimes more than a thousand years old, is a spiritual being. The finished canoe is given a name and launched with a ceremony. When it is worn out and needs to be replaced, the old bow piece is sometimes added onto a new canoe so as to continue the life of the previous vessel.

Today the experience of carving a canoe has changed, but the essential aspects of respect and ceremony remain. The demands of time in our modern world and the use of power tools have had both positive and negative effects. The canoe is a very sophisticated and highly evolved marine vessel. Building a traditional canoe involves thorough research of the old canoes in public collections, as well as talking with the handful of canoe builders who learned from their families. There are many subtle yet important aspects of canoe construction that cannot be learned only through building. For example, the canoe starts to taper to bow slightly behind the halfway point, making the widest point of the vessel actually closer to the stern. The way the canoe enters or cuts through the water is just as important as the way it exits at the stern. How the canoe interacts with the water from the cutwater at the bow to the exit at the stern will dictate the efficiency of the vessel. The sides of a canoe are another example; they do not come up straight to the top of the gunwales, but flare outwards in a graceful arc, which helps keep water from spilling over them. The flat bar of the chain saw has influenced some contemporary carvers to straighten out lines that were previously curved, but it is the responsibility of the artist to guide the tools rather than letting the tools dictate to him or her. Elbow adzes and D-adzes are still the main tools in canoe construction.

Some things have changed of necessity. Historically, the top and bottom of a canoe were determined by floating a log in the water. The dense portion, being heavier, would naturally roll to the underside, becoming the bottom of the canoe. Today we often get our cedar from logging companies; it sits in a booming yard, the top drying in the sun, making the age-old test invalid. Though we work more quickly with today's tools, we also have much less time. The old-timers built their canoes over two seasons, and there was always community help. We work to deadlines today, and fund-raising is often required. But the essential aspects of canoe building remain as they have always been.

*Andrew (Wouldhe) Tait blesses the cedar log for David Neel's canoe using sage
and an eagle feather fan.*

The rebirth of the canoe is catching for those of us who get close to it. At the closing ceremonies of Tribal Journeys, in the Mungo Martin bighouse in Victoria, I formally accepted the challenge to participate in the La Push paddle in 1997. With the support of my family, I will make the journey in my own canoe.

I began my canoe for traditional use by my family, and I conceived it as a project I would undertake on my own. I felt that if my ancestor, Charlie James, could carve sixty-foot totem poles with only one good hand, I could manage a twenty-five-foot canoe. In addition, one of my elders advised me that fund-raising and money worries detract from the spiritual aspects of building a canoe. I decided to go ahead, after much soul-searching, because I feel it is important to pursue your dreams. This idealism was to cause me much mental anguish as the time came to begin carving and the project seemed overwhelming.

The first step was to secure an old-growth Western red cedar. This was done with the generosity of the Ehattesaht First Nation and of MacMillan Bloedel, who donated a log. I journeyed to Elk River, where I had my pick of the logs in the booming ground. The folks there suggested a beautiful thirty-four-foot cedar, which was an appropriate size for my canoe. But I had my eye on an incredible forty-one-foot log that was over six feet in diameter at the butt end and probably twelve hundred years old. It was such a grand old tree; there is truly something magical about a tree that has lived that long on our earth. But as I awaited its delivery to my carving site in Campbell River and continued to discuss the project with other carvers, I began to realize that, with the larger log, I would end up with a huge amount of wood to remove. And by cutting away this exterior wood I would be establishing the sides of the canoe deeper in the tree, where there would be branches and knots. So I decided on the smaller tree after all. On a sunny July day it was delivered to my site overlooking Discovery Passage on northern Vancouver Island.

With the help of Chief Russell Quocksistalis and Andrew (Wouldhe) Tait, I arranged a blessing ceremony to prepare the log for the transformation into a traditional ocean-going craft. The log was smudged and the ashes later deposited in the river. Under the cover of the Foreshore Bighouse, a song was sung and I danced a *K'sala*, the wind and rain howling from the southeast. Chief Quocksistalis told of the meaning of what we were doing, and who my family was that I came to be carving this canoe. My father, David Neel Sr., was a carver who had been trained by his mother, Ellen Neel, and her uncle Mungo Martin. Ellen was one of the first woman carvers on the coast, I am told; carving is historically passed down from father to son, and Ellen was one of the first women to break the pattern, under the training of her grandfather Charlie James, the great master. Once the ceremony was over, I was free to begin my formidable task.

A five-hundred-year-old cedar, measuring thirty-four feet by three feet, looks like a lot of project to jump into as it sits on the ground before you. Fortunately my friend Mervyn Child, from my home village of Fort Rupert, had done two canoes, and he helped me saw off the big wood, revealing the form of a canoe within. With the two of us manning the saw and two others helping out, we had it shaped like a canoe in two days. Milling the wood from this grandfather log required a chain saw with a six-foot bar, with Mervyn at one end and me at the other. One thing that anyone will notice in working with cedar is the wonderful aroma of the wood. Cedar contains thujaplicin, a natural oil that is an excellent preservative, one of the reasons the wood is so well suited to totem poles, bighouses and canoes. The work slowed down considerably after this roughing-out stage, and I was on my own.

Before I began working I had interviewed approximately fifty people involved with building or using canoes, visited museums and studied many canoes in the water. But I was to find that the process of sculpting a canoe can only be understood by doing it. Once wood is removed, it cannot be replaced. To avoid errors and make the best use of the log, careful planning and visualization are necessary. Mervyn's favourite axiom, "Measure twice, cut once," proved invaluable. The carver needs to be thinking about what his or her canoe will look like after each step, as well as having an image of the final product. Steaming changes the lines dramatically. This makes it all the more difficult to project the shape of the finished craft.

The actual building of the canoe was a lot more labour than I had ever anticipated. I completed a plan of the top and side views, which gave me a guide to follow. But I found that once I had made my initial cuts and the major wood was removed, I preferred to use my own vision and intuition, looking at photographs and measurements taken from old canoes. The process became one more of sculpting than construction. As the wood came away, the many bits of advice and pointers from the people I had interviewed echoed in my ears.

Under the steady fall of my elbow adze my canoe took shape, straight saw cuts becoming flowing curves. The goal is to have each curve, each angle, flow into the next, into an overall form that has no beginning and no end but is simply a series of sophisticated sweeps with its roots in the past. Achieving these old-world sculptural ideals while dealing with the contemporary realities of family, economic and personal demands proved difficult. I was to realize that the biggest challenge in sculpting my canoe was simply finding the time to do it. As the summer sun faded into the fall breeze, I became more anxious. I fully realized that my ability, and my eagerness, to work on the dugout would wane as the cold and wet settled in. Trips to Santa Fe, Vancouver and New York were interspersed with periods of creative labour, but slowly the age-old design took form. I would take pleasure in standing back and looking at the canoe to see how its lines flowed, imagining it a foot higher once the pieces had been added to the bow and stern. I gave it dramatic lines, befitting a larger craft, but that is the way I saw it in my mind's eye.

A canoe, through all the phases of its life, from construction to travel, brings people together. My carving site, in a public park, became a spot for both locals and tourists to visit. It was not unusual for visitors from England, Japan and Germany to stop by during the course of an afternoon's work. At one point a weary traveller even brought in bedding and proceeded to live under my canoe. I decided to allow him to share in the canoe experience, and he stayed for about two weeks, until I flipped the canoe over.

When the work was finally complete and I ran my eyes over the sleek form of the family canoe, I experienced a peace inside. I could feel the energy, the knowledge and the responsibility of the carvers who came before me. When I laid my hands on the gunwales, I could tell that something very important was coming back to me, my family and my people.

Like Haida artist Bill Reid, I believe the traditional canoe to be the basis for Northwest Coast design and sculptural principles. The canoe's form, the way each line flows and interacts, follows the same principles as those employed when carving a mask or painting a housefront. The canoe is very sophisticated in its construction and function, slicing cleanly through waves, its high stern pushing it along in a following sea. In spirit it is kinetic sculpture: art designed to navigate the sea under the pull of the paddle. Contained within the canoe is the essence of our artform, as well as the combined knowledge of our old people, transported into this period of our history for us to breathe life into once again. To paddle a dugout is to be affected by it. The canoe retains a spirit once encased in a living body hundreds of years old. The teaching says that we, the people of the Northwest Pacific Coast, are people of the cedar. Along with the salmon, the cedar is the basis for our traditional culture. It is as though this sacred vessel has been sent by our ancestors to guide us into an uncertain future.

David Neel with family and friends following the blessing of the log ceremony for his canoe.
Back row, left to right: *Mark Racalma, Sharon Neel, David Neel, Andrew (Wouldhe) Tait, Russell Quocksistalis*
Front row: *Louise Hungar* (left) *and Alvin Neel*

Only five or ten years ago the canoe, like many of our traditions, seemed destined to be a part of our rich past. Today its continuation is assured. Physically it is the same vessel, but its function has evolved. It returns to us carrying the knowledge and pride of our ancestors. We continue to carve canoes, as we always have, from the red cedar. Many of the trees that supply us with our canoes were already hundreds of years old when the first tall ships came to our shores. In their lifetimes these trees have seen a new people settle upon the land, seen our Native populations diminish, seen the canoe become a memory, and then be reborn again in a modern world. With contemporary forest practices, will our grandchildren have old-growth cedar to continue our traditions? And what role will these wise giants play in a world of global economies, television and space travel? How will we nourish in our youth the respect that we feel, having seen the great canoe return to our people?

The heroes of many of our stories go into the forest, or to the depths of the ocean, to find upon their return that they have been away not days but years. Like our canoes, they return transformed, with great gifts to share with the people. I am told all the knowledge to building a canoe is within the tree itself. Perhaps some of the answers for our people are held within the canoe, or the journey of the canoe. Where the journey will take us we cannot yet see. But like a trusted horse that guides its rider in times of difficulty, the canoe will continue to guide us. In a world of mortgages and deadlines it can be difficult to have faith in spiritual and cultural values. For myself, and for many others on the journey, the canoe is an important physical symbol for the relevance of the ways of our ancestors. Our families and our nations have left us many gifts that can benefit us even today, but reaping these benefits requires great effort. Will the canoe tradition be alive and flourishing in ten years' time? Will our children understand its importance and practise our traditions so that our grandchildren will have them? These are important questions to ask as you read through the words of the people of the great canoes.

THE GREAT
CANOES

MARY McQUILLEN
KWE-DE-CHE-AUTLH
Port Townsend, Washington Born 1932

When they began to get involved with canoes again I first helped my son to learn the protocol and to know his history thoroughly. When I joined the group going to Bella Bella on the support crew I found that no one knew how to properly come into a village and other protocol. How to show respect for the people and for the chiefs of the village. And more importantly how to be thankful for the tree, and to show respect for the water, so that the water would be helpful to them. So after we stopped paddling we would have a prayer right away, then after we took care of the canoe and our gear it was time to join the festivities. Each evening we would have a circle, so no one would bring any bad feelings into the canoe the next day. The canoe feels everything; the water feels everything, my grandfather used to say. The discipline and the prayer were very important. We took care of each other like a family. We made sure that for each one that travelled with us, our spiritual life was intact. We prayed for everyone even if we were upset; in this way we could travel in a good way. This way the canoe would take care of us, because it knows what we are feeling.

I learned from my grandfather. I grew up with all men; my mother died when I was young and I had no aunts, so I was under the care of my uncles and grandfather. It just worked out that I was always there when it came to the canoe. We had to show respect to the water, to the salmon and everything that the Creator sent us. We would respect the cedar that gave its life for our canoe, the salmon that gave its life so we could eat. We show our respect through prayer, fasting and prayer songs; this is our tradition. My brothers were taught these things also. A lot of people moved away from our culture for a long time. There were just a few families that hung onto their songs and traditions. My grandfather taught me the songs, and he told me if I ever forgot my songs we would lose our history. We're ocean-going people. Our ancestors were whalers, but now we don't hunt the whale, and the salmon is almost gone. There used to be hundreds of canoes in our villages. I used to go fishing in our canoe. After we had gas boats, they'd tow ten of us or so in our canoes tied all in a row, out to the fishing grounds. We'd use sealing canoes for fishing in those days. This was in the 1950s. We had some pretty rough waters. One by one we started losing our canoes. They would get busted up on the beach; the wood became harder to get. There are no old canoes in our village any more. We still have people who can carve canoes. ▸

Facing page: Chief Henry George, Gwa'sala'Nakwaxda'xw, makes a formal welcome speech on behalf of his people at Bella Bella, B.C.

*Geronimo Jones of the Port Gamble S'Klallam Nation at the Healing of the Waters ceremony,
Olympia, Washington.*

Gerald Stewart, Tsimshian, a member of the Spirit of the North Wind crew, stands in Bill Reid's LooPlex *at Clam Beach, B.C.*

But we don't have any big trees left, only in the parks. Logging companies have cleared about everything around this area.

I really think the canoe is important today. We need to have different forms of transportation again. So much oil has been pumped out of the earth, and other resources; now we need to return to some of the traditions again to help the earth recover. Only the Creator can make the earth recover, but we can help. It will take a long time, but it took us a long time to get to Bella Bella, and it was worth it. When you paddle you have to be in good shape: your mind, spirit and body. It's a discipline that we have gotten away from. We have to have the discipline of the old people.

BOBBY BAKER
SQUAMISH
North Vancouver, B.C. Born 1946

Ocean-going canoes have always been a fascination of mine. I've been involved with our racing and sailing canoes in Squamish territory ever since I was a young kid. When I lived in Hawaii for a while I got involved with Polynesian canoes. So it was just a natural thing when I returned to the Northwest Coast to get involved with canoes again, and when I noticed that there wasn't any ocean-going canoes available to our nation I proceeded to get one built. I proceeded to lobby our council, our chiefs, our people, and more or less sold the idea, the vision, that our involvement in sea-going cultural exercises is very vital to our nation. We're city Indians down here in Vancouver. We're losing a lot of our traditions, our culture, our language. With this rebirth of ocean-going canoes, this coming to the surface again, we can identify what our culture is, and our traditions.

The canoe is a sacred vessel. The canoe is a living entity that provides you with not just transportation but the experience of moving over water and through time. The canoe is special, a special being, and you can sense it. Each different canoe has its own spirit. You get into one canoe and it feels a certain way, you get into another canoe and it feels another way, you get into our canoe and it feels a certain way. We're all proud of these different ways of our canoes, the canoe's spirit. The canoe is not just a boat, it's part of the family.

We prepared for our journey to Qatuwas in every way we could possibly think of that was at our disposal: sweatlodge ceremonies every Saturday for about three months prior to leaving our ▸

Facing page: *The maiden voyage of the Weiwaikum Nation canoe,* ƛ'uinequala *(Lightning Speed).*

home territory; swims in the Capilano River to strengthen us up, to give us more power. We were out in the canoe three times a week for short stretches. We pulled a bucket behind the canoe to strengthen ourselves. We met every Monday night for the first couple of months to brainstorm, socialize and gain proper focus as to what the journey would encompass. We did a lot of preparation. So when it came to the actual journey we came out of there like we just got shot out of a cannon. We couldn't wait to get out into the wilderness and test out all our theories and how we thought things would be. Cedric Billy and myself carved the canoe. He is a racing canoe carver. It was a really good experience. I like working with the cedar.

When we came into other villages along the way the reception was very high-spirited, very welcoming and loving. They really opened up to us. They knew they wanted us, but they didn't know how much, and vice versa. It was really emotional times and joyous times being involved with other villages as we came through and stopped in their territories.

I think the canoe has a place in the modern world. We're water people. Just as sure as the plains people need their horses, water people need their canoes. That's the way our ancestors intended. Let's take these traditional tools that they've given us and exercise them. We will learn, we will experience the teachings that they have put here for us. That's what the canoe is: an instrument. We use it and we learn. Everybody who has used their canoe has learned something about their ancestors: their experiences, how they felt, the hardships, the anticipation, the excitement in going someplace in the canoe and the necessity to prepare. I see this as a growing tradition; we're just laying the foundation. This is something that we will use to strengthen us. This is the medicine it takes to make ourselves better. This cultural exercise will support our nation in the sense it will be something that we will be able to stand on top of, we'll have it under our belts. We'll be able to move forward because we've become something; we've become people who realize what needs to be done in our future traditionally, culturally and spiritually. So we have gained a lot.

Detail of the Kwaiwna *(Steelhead), the canoe of the La Push Nation.*

BILL REID

HAIDA

Vancouver, B.C. Born 1920

Nobody comes around to ask me about canoes, although I was one of the first to start building a proper canoe, a few years back. Some have the attitude, "I'm an Indian, I don't have to learn how, to be able to carve a canoe." There's a lot involved in building a canoe.

I started studying the canoes in museums, then began by building a model. I started by building a small canoe, and later did a fifty-footer. We did pretty well; we've never shipped any water in the *LooTaas*.

There wasn't anyone really doing canoes when I got started. There was a lot of published material, though you did have to sort through it. A lot of it is wrong. One anthropologist I read suggested steaming a canoe for two days! There are canoes in museum collections also. The Haida canoe in the American Museum of Natural History is actually built backwards. The bow of the canoe is carved from the butt of the log, where it is supposed to be the reverse. That very large canoe would be for ceremonial use. On those big canoes, the stern should be higher than the prow by about six inches, because the trouble with navigating those big vessels is in a following sea. With those war canoes in the old days most of the fighting was done with paddles; that's why the paddles are pointed. The reason is, when they were navigating the boat, they wouldn't have had time to change weapons.

Canoe walls tend to be thin, about seven-eighths of an inch thick. The bottom needs to be about two inches thick. A canoe is not really structurally sound until you steam it. It gains strength. Steaming really affects the way the canoe acts in the water. Before it's steamed the canoe rolls from side to side, like a log. When you steam it, it becomes more like a boat. What happens is, when the canoe is steamed it makes the sides displace more water, so when it rolls on its side it wants to roll back upright. The whole shape is changed in steaming.

Something I saw Mungo Martin use is a lofting stick. It bends, and you use it to measure your curves. Different-length sticks are used for various parts of the canoe. Because it's flexible, the stick can be bent along the side of the canoe, and templates can be made to match one side of the canoe to the other.

Facing page: *Technology has quickened the canoe-building process, but the fundamental tools remain the elbow adze, the D-adze and various carving knives.*

Mervyn Child, Kwakwaka'wakw,
puts the finishing touches on
the Comox Nation canoe, I-Hos,
in the Comox bighouse.

GUUJAAW
RAVEN CLAN, QAGYALKIIGIWAAY (SKIDANS)
Masset, B.C.

As the ice age receded, our people lived in tundra conditions using grasses for shelter and warmth. The Xagi town people witnessed and adopted the first tree as their crest. At the great gatherings after that they tied branches in their hair to celebrate and remember the first tree. We know now that the first tree arrived on Haida Gwaii about 14,000 years ago. As the other trees arrived, so did the cedar, only about 6,000 years ago.

There was a time when our people pushed logs off the shore with their fishing gear hung from them. They survived the last flood on rafts.

Eventually people travelled about in crude little dugout canoes. The "Northwest" canoe shape that we think about didn't come about until much later. A man went into the forest to find a tree to build his dugout. He felled a tree and built a camp out of cedar bark. After he had bedded down for the night, he heard a chopping sound from where his tree was laid out. He did not go to investigate until morning. When he looked at his log, it was carved to the gunwale and he knew it was the work of the mysterious people. He observed and remembered what he saw. In the following nights, more work was carried out, step by step, in the same fashion, and he remembered. This went on, taking the man through the whole canoe-building process and the canoe that we recognize as the Northwest Coast canoe today. This happened in Juskatla Inlet.

Canoes were traded out of Masset Inlet as far north as the Chilkat River and south into Kwakwaka'wakw country.

The old people knew their stuff, and they got around, too. We blueprinted an old twenty-seven-foot canoe, and it was accurate to within one-sixtieth of an inch. It's pretty good if a boat builder is that close even today.

Over the years we've been locating old canoes in the bush that were abandoned at different stages due to the pestilence that struck our people. Like the first guy who was shown the canoe-making process, the different stages for getting to the final form soon became apparent. So far we've found about twenty of them, as well as hundreds of stumps and tops from which canoes had been taken. Around these canoe sites we also find holes where people looked into the heart of the cedar for soundness. Bark stripping, for any of the numerous reasons, can still be seen. Many of ▸

Detail of the Comox Nation canoe, I-Hos, *showing how bad sections of wood are repaired. Damaged or rotted wood is carved away, and a tightly fitting plug is glued and pegged into place.*

Canoes in progress at Alert Bay, B.C.

Bill Henderson, Weiwaikum, uses a traditional curved knife to put the finishing touches on a canoe prow.

these trees are still alive and growing, as living links to the old people. There's a tree with yew wood wedges to spit off planks still standing as they left it.

Sometimes we find bits of the scaffolding that was built to get above the flare. We found out that small canoes were built with the butt of the tree at the stern, while the big canoes had the prow at the butt. You realize why when you observe the performance of the different-sized canoes in a following sea.

Another thing that puzzled us for a while was a shallow hollow the whole length of the canoe, before the main hollowing out. We eventually figured out that it was the water level, which enabled the canoe maker to loft it true.

The keystone to the canoe-making formula was remembered by Alfred Davidson and Adam Bell, who had seen canoes built in their youth at Masset. At transition point between the belly and the hollow is a V. This is the strength of the canoe, and all lines fair through it. Otherwise there would be no reference, and the steaming wouldn't work.

When a canoe is carved, the canoe maker knows that the final shape comes after steaming. As the canoe gets wider it also pulls shorter. As the sides get pushed out and down, the ends lift, giving the bottom a gentle rocker. Without it, the performance would be stiff, and the canoe would be almost impossible to turn. As the sides push out and down, the belly is slightly flattened at the hip, building in stability. In all, about twelve things happen all in one movement during steaming, resulting in a graceful sight to behold and one of the finest and most ingenious maritime vessels of all time.

A person shouldn't even think of building a canoe if he isn't ready to go "without" for a while. The old people obviously knew what they were doing, and I don't think they added these rules just to get it done faster. A canoe demands your undivided attention, and a canoe gets jealous.

There are politics, of course. We don't have to say much other than that suitable cedar trees are getting scarce. In the second growth they expect to cut the trees in sixty or seventy years. A canoe log must be four hundred to eight hundred years old. The choice is simple: Let them have their way with the land, or we look after the sacred workplaces of our ancestors.

Facing page: *The Squamish canoe,* Kxwu7lh, *at Olympia, Washington.*

The crew of the Maxwalogwa *trade stories and talk about canoe building at Clam Beach, B.C.*

The sun momentarily breaks through the clouds as canoes come ashore at Pauquachin, B.C., during the Tribal Journeys paddle.

Overleaf: *The ƛ'uinequala is launched into the waters of Discovery Passage. It was the first time a traditional dugout had been used in the area for about seventy-five years.*

SIMON DICK

NAKWAXDA'XW (BLUNDEN HARBOUR)

Port Hardy, B.C. Born 1951

I got started in canoes back in 1985. Bill Reid got a commission to build a canoe and he hired Gary Edenshaw (Guujaaw). His budget allowed him to hire a helper, too, and I happened to be there. We started working together, and it was like a trial and error thing. The Museum of Anthropology at the University of British Columbia trucked in a twelve-foot Haida canoe that was well over a hundred years old from Ottawa. We took the lines off that and applied it to a twenty-five-footer, and later Bill Reid took the lines off the twenty-five-footer and put them on the *LooTaas,* stretching it twice again to fifty feet.

What we're seeing is a resurrection of knowledge, but in these modern times it will be trial and error again. Because of the high energy of chain saws and power planers, it can come to a point where it's quite dangerous if a master carver isn't really on top of his crew. Sometimes there's two or three chain saws on a site at the same time. The crew could overlook what they're supposed to do, get carried away and lose some wood, cut too deep. In the early days it was different. I can't begin to imagine how long it took them in the early days, just with hand saws and axes and adzes. They'd have to burn out the middle to hollow it out. It would be a matter of months. Usually they would carve canoes in the moist months; in the summer the wood would get too dry and brittle. They were too busy anyway harvesting in the summer.

I was raised in canoes in Kingcome Inlet. I always had a love for canoes. We used to borrow my grandfather's canoe all the time to go trout fishing, or to go hunting, or to go check the net. We always played in canoes. It was my dream that someday I would build one, and I have. In some areas, like in Kingcome, canoes were used as recently as twenty years ago. River canoes, not ocean-going canoes. There are still old-time canoe builders around. They're not physically active, but as consultants and directors they're still active. In Kingcome there's still a few who witnessed, participated, directed and actually constructed their own canoes. I have a couple uncles who are quite knowledged in canoe construction. And before I do a canoe I always use them as consultants.

It's really important to be in touch with the spiritual essence of doing a canoe; it should not be simply construction. First of all it means being clean and sober, not abusing alcohol. And bathing in the creek or in the ocean every day, fasting, keeping yourself clear. ▸

Facing page: *The Elwha S'Klallam canoe,* Warrior, *anchored out with fishing boats at Bella Bella, B.C.*

Cheryl Rivers, Squamish, carries the Queen's Baton into Cowichan, B.C.,
on the Tribal Journeys paddle to Victoria.

The revival of the canoe is important because we're ocean-going people. This ocean is our highway, our lifeline, our bloodline. One of my uncles said to me, "Nowadays we have roads and highways; in the early days our canoes parked there, that was our Rolls Royce, Chevrolet or Ford." Everybody had their own model, their own design. They all went for the elegance and the speed, the majestic-looking canoes. It was quite competitive. Canoes were given names immediately, with ceremonies: like a person, they're a living thing. They're cared for with great respect.

I estimate this log for our canoe to be well over seven hundred years old. It's hard to imagine seven hundred years ago it was just a little seedling somewhere. It has granted me so much pride to see the youth paddle the canoe. For them it's a dream come true, and the level of appreciation and self-esteem of these young people to me is truly a gift from the Creator. They are really, really proud of themselves, and that makes me proud and that makes me happy. It's a level of happiness that we're finding in ourselves again that our ancestors had. I see this tradition growing, not just for festivals, but to go to potlatches, ceremonies, just to travel. Why take the highway when you can take the straits?

MICHAEL HUNT
NAMGIS
Alert Bay, B.C. Born 1974

The paddle to the Commonwealth Games was my second canoe journey. I'm involved because it touches the inside of me to learn about my culture. No one really taught me about my culture, and I'm starting to learn about it slowly. On journeys like this I meet a lot of people and learn about different cultures. You learn a lot when you're pulling, because they sing songs and they talk the language.

Pulling is a hard thing to do, but when you get into it... Some people in their first year are really sore, but if you continue it gets better. You've just got to be in really good shape to do it. It requires knowledge to paddle a canoe. I'm going to keep paddling, then when I have children I'm going to pass it on to them, so they can say, "Well, my father did this, 'cause my grandfather and my great-grandfather did this." So I'm carrying it on for other generations. I got everyone to sign my paddle, and I'm going to be handing it on to my children. It's a great feeling to have this paddle and ▸

travel to different nations. It's just beautiful. I was crying when I came into Victoria, happy tears.

Being sober and drug-free is very important in paddling canoe. While I was back home that's all I did, that was my famous thing to do, drink and do drugs. I feel a lot better; I feel like a human being. I went to a treatment centre for six weeks and I really looked at myself and I finally know who I am. I have trouble reading. A couple years ago I was ashamed when somebody asked me to read, and I was too ashamed to say it. Now I can just come out and say that I don't know how to read. I'm an honest guy now; I never used to be honest. If something's on my mind I'll tell you about it. So these trips make you think and have an open mind, because that's what they teach you out there. Actually you teach yourself, because you have to have an open mind to do things. Like I was scared to go up and sing and dance; last year they told me just to go up. You don't have to be asked, just go up and do it. Have an open mind and go for it.

TOM ABEL
HAIDA
Kuna, Alaska Born 1947

We're ocean people, and the way I've been told Haidas are from the spirit of the ocean. When I first met my relative Morris White in 1976, the major topic of our conversation was canoes. There were none at that time in Masset. Our conversation was built around when he was going to make canoes, and when we would eventually bring those canoes to Hydaburg. That's where my interest in canoes really began.

I am happy and proud to say I was one of the people who helped organize the Paddle to Hydaburg. I talked to the elders in Hydaburg and I asked them all, "Have you ever seen a canoe?" And they all said, "No." And I said, "Would you like to see a canoe?" And they all said, "Yes." And about three-fourths of them were crying with emotion. So I said, "We're going to do it!" We did it, and it was difficult. We called up Skidegate, and we invited the *LooTaas* to come over. And I ended up calling up Morris White and asked him to come over. In the space of about two weeks we raised ten thousand dollars to pay insurance and all the incidentals. It was a very moving experience, and the reason we did it was we wanted our old people to see a canoe before they died; also for the symbolic unification of our peoples across the U.S./Canada border, which we didn't create between ourselves. ▶

Facing page: *Detail of a Coast Salish canoe prow. More than any other aspect of canoe building, the carving of the prow allows the carver to express an individual vision.*

*A young Haida girl stops to watch Heiltsuk chiefs during the
Qatuwas welcoming ceremony.*

Before the border, people from Masset used to come to Hydaburg every single year. They say they used to sit across the bay in Hydaburg and sing the night before they landed. They'd tie all the boats together, make a dance platform and sing and dance all night. Then in the morning they'd make their official entrance. When the border became more of a serious matter between Canada and the U.S., it became no longer a reality that people could just come from Masset to Hydaburg.

When those canoes first came to Hydaburg in 1989, everyone on that beach cried, except a few of us that forced ourselves not to. It made us yearn for what was ours. The canoe symbolized our strength, our life and our means of gathering food, travelling to meet with each other and also interacting with other tribes all up and down the coast. They were our economic vehicles. And they are a very, very wonderful political weapon nowadays. When they came across from Masset, they brought across a traditional chief who is also a Mountie. He said, "When we came to the border, we circled two times; we looked at the water and there was no black line, so we came on." To me that's highly symbolic of the attitude: no dividing line on the water between our people. All it took to erase that line was two canoes full of Haidas, coming from Masset with nothing on them but a paddle and a Haida passport. The political implications of that are very far-reaching.

This canoe gathering, Qatuwas, is a very powerful political message to the world that our people are unifying and that we're using our canoes as a symbol of our sovereignty. That's why they're so precious to me, because of what they symbolize; they symbolize our life, our sovereign right, our strength and power.

CHIEF FRANK NELSON
MUSGAMA
Victoria, B.C. Born 1945

I worked as the cultural co-ordinator for the Native Participation Committee for the 1994 Commonwealth Games, helping co-ordinate the Tribal Journeys canoe expedition. I believe very much in the resurgence of our canoe nations. When I was working with the committee I saw early on that there was an opportunity to commit ourselves to a healing path for our children.

I believe that the canoe is a step back into our history, that we once more conjure up all of the images that's associated with our forefathers. I now know that there's a different feeling as you sit

Previous page: *Frank Brown, Heiltsuk, was the organizer of the*
1993 Qatuwas Festival.

in a canoe and then as you pull, the euphoric feeling as you're paddling. It gives you time to reflect on our history as the First Nations people. And somehow we come up with an effort, individually and jointly, to seek a new direction. I think that's important at this stage in our lives so that we can begin to be positive about the things that we need to do for our children.

There are a lot of canoes now, and it's phenomenal the impact that it has. The people that were honoured to depart first on this journey to Victoria were the Oweekeno (Rivers Inlet) people. They built their canoe specifically to be a part of this journey, and that says a lot for a small community. They pulled together, and they accomplished a major feat in their lives.

The canoe plays an important role today. To me it is very spiritual just to be able to be a part of it, and to once more travel and become attuned to our surroundings. It contains all the history of our people.

CHRIS MORGANROTH
QUILEUTE
La Push, Washington Born 1939

I got started in canoes when I was a very young boy. My grandpa started taking me in a canoe when I was five years old, to gather materials for baskets. Used to go up the river to gather cedar bark and straw. Because my people were fishing people they relied on the canoes for many years until the introduction of various other boats and outboard motors, then you can see the change. I don't think it was a cultural change. It was a change to be competitive, because people wanted to get more fish; the faster they could get them the better. Canoes were still being built. I used to watch the canoe builders. Some people say they differed a lot here and there, with various builders. But I think they all had the same basic perception of what a canoe was, and what it should look like, and different things connected with building your canoe, such as spirituality and why a canoe was built the way it was. Why certain things were carved on a canoe.

Purity was important. The implements in the canoe, everything has spiritual connections. This is why they put the "heart" into the canoe. The heart was to give it the life, because the canoe was sometimes the guide. In difficult times, in a storm, at nighttime when they couldn't see where they were going, they had to rely on their spiritual connections between each other to make sure they ▶

45

Brad Roberts, Weiwaikum, uses an elbow adze to hollow out the X̱'quinequala.

were guided in the right direction. Therefore life had to be in the canoe. And of course, a heart has more meaning than just having a brain. It means that there is a closer relationship, because love comes from the heart, and you feel that close relationship with everything that you got, such as a canoe, a harpoon, a paddle or the various things that you bring with you. All the things that are there, everything has spiritual connections. Respect is very important. If there is disrespect, you are very unlikely to be successful in anything you do for the good of people. If you have disrespect for a cedar tree, or disrespect for the whale or the salmon, and you abuse it, it's not going to do you any good, or anybody else.

A canoe's heart is usually a protrusion carved into the bow, with the stripes carved from below the ears of the wolf head. Sometimes they're curved, sometimes they're straight from the top edge of what we know as the gunwales or the rail of the canoe. And also the eyes are incorporated, using two eyes on each side, to make sure that the canoe knows where it's going. I think all the Salish and many of the Nuu-chah-nulth peoples had similar canoes. The people used to go trade on south Vancouver Island and sometimes some of the larger canoes were fifty to sixty feet long. A big canoe like that is not very practical. They were hard to care for. They had very specific uses, like travelling with many people or moving a lot of people around at one time, maybe even a war canoe. It was easier to use a smaller canoe; they were faster in the water. In my teachings the larger canoes ended up being used as gifts.

The canoe had its very important meaning to the people because it got them to different places to go hunting, to go fishing, to go visit, to have ceremony, you name it. The canoe was the most important thing to be able to live, because whenever the seasons permitted they would go out to the ocean.

If it were not for the cedar tree the culture wouldn't be so well developed as it is today, because the cedar tree brought many different things to the people, not just houses and canoes but clothing and baskets; such a wide variety came from the cedar tree. There are canoes that have been made out of Alaskan yellow cedar, and there are canoes that have been made out of spruce. Cedar had more quality; it was stronger, it had the straight grain, it was inherent with the oils that made it last. You don't see that kind of oil in the newer trees where they are growing faster. The old-growth trees are preferred for the canoe because of the tighter grains and the oils that are in there.

When I hear a canoe referred to as a boat, I get insulted. With a boat there is no spiritual connection. With the canoe at one time the whole thing was living, and you can see, you can touch ▶

Overleaf: *Chuck Sam, Squamish, cares for the* Ḵxwu7lh
at the end of a day's paddle.

the canoe, you touch the paths of people. You touch a boat and there is no feeling there, just nails, fiberglass, screws, paint. It doesn't have any real meaning. You know that your history is written in the canoe somewhere, not just you, but your people.

I helped build canoes when I was very young. I watched a lot being built, so I learned that when you build a canoe you use your eye and hand and leave it alone for a while and let it tell you, "This is the way I should be." You just carve, and your hand has to go on the right places. Sometimes the canoe builder that's only interested in making profit would make a very light canoe and make the canoe bottom thin. A thin-bottom canoe don't last. A proper canoe bottom should be up to four inches thick, they call it four fingers thick.

When we rebuilt our canoe we just took our time. I know of people that built canoes in three or six weeks or something like that. I guess I am a little different. When I build something, I like to see something graceful and beautiful come out of it and I like to take my time, stand back and look and see. Because when you stand back and look and see you're less apt to make a mistake. I think there is a real historical significance in this canoe, which was built by Conrad Williams in 1928. I think that the future canoes of the tribe is going to depend on the configuration of how that one was built. The pattern, the size, everything about it. They will look at it and say, This was a good canoe and we need to build another one like it. There is nothing wrong with replicating or duplicating; I think it's important.

The timber industry is taking more and more of a toll on the availability of logs of the size that we need. They are few and far between now, no matter where you go. Even if you go into an old-growth forest, you have to fight the public or the powers that be over the piece of land where that timber is growing, in order to get that tree for your cultural purposes. It's mainly because society today is too dependent on many of the resources. The salmon, the trees: we just don't have the things that we had, say, a hundred years ago or even fifty. You can see there is a diminishing salmon run because of environmental degradation and the size of the harvest going on, too few fish for too many people. So in that respect the resource has been diminishing rapidly.

When you see a canoe you see my past and my history, and I don't want that to be lost, my culture. So it has a very, very, unique place in today's world. We believe that we have, we have had in the past, a more mindful awareness of the resources, and we see some great losses happening. If the last cedar tree is cut down our culture dies also.

LELA MAY MORGANROTH

QUILEUTE

La Push, Washington Born 1937

I've been involved in a couple of canoe journeys. I was on the Paddle to Seattle as ground crew. Travelling in our canoe we're doing it as our ancestors did it a long time ago, and it gives us more spirit and power through our hearts and through our minds, and it changes a lot of people. The trip is drug and alcohol free. There's a lot of people who really changed their life around, really got into this paddling and doing their traditional ways.

I'm a Quileute Indian, and I've done a lot of things in the traditional ways. I seen a lot of people one time, when I was six years old, they came in their canoes on the Quileute River, and I seen big chiefs come in there and they got on their apple-box stand and started making speeches, and they had their regalia and their potlatch songs. It was really great. They dressed up in their cedar bark outfit, or they dressed in what their tribes used. It was a lot different than today's world.

Overleaf: *Masked Kwak'waka'wakw dancers perform in the bows of their canoes as they enter Victoria's inner harbour at the close of Tribal Journeys.*

PEGGY AHVAKANA
SUQUAMISH
Suquamish, Washington Born 1948

In 1989 there was the Paddle to Seattle, and during that time Frank Brown made a challenge to the Pacific Rim canoe people to come to Bella Bella. At the time the Suquamish didn't have a canoe. We never dreamed that we could ever do it; there was no real base of knowledge, no cultural foundation to get such a big task done. A Duwamish elder mentioned that at the Center for Wooden Boats in Seattle there was a canoe. Zeke Zahir went to have a look at it. It had been carved by Sherwood Martin and a group of schoolkids under the guidance of a Duwamish man in the 1970s. We began to realize that we had access to a canoe, and we then began to talk seriously about the journey. We met at the beach during Chief Seattle Days in 1992; we talked to whoever would listen, and that day I decided to go to Bella Bella. From that group three of us went on the trip: Frank Fowler, who became the captain, his wife, Zoe, and myself. I was the cultural development specialist for my tribe, and I told my supervisor I was going on this trip to Bella Bella even if I had to quit my job. We ended up putting in an Administration for Native Americans grant and the Suquamish went to Bella Bella.

We asked Sherwood Martin if we could use his canoe for the journey. He said it needed a lot of repair. Jeff Carriere and his father, Ed, took the canoe to their carving shed, where they did the work that needed to be done. All the work was done on a volunteer basis. Frank and Jeff quit their jobs in order to make this trip.

I knew that Bella Bella was important; I didn't know how important at the time. I saw it as a vehicle for recapturing some of the Suquamish culture that was lost and dormant for so many years. I've always been interested in revitalizing the culture and bringing back as much as we can. I saw that trip as the only way, not only to participate in my own culture but to be part of a much larger culture that I'd only heard of. I'd only heard of the longhouses, the dances, the songs; here at Suquamish, it was decimated. The Bella Bella journey, it definitely changed lives. During that one trip, we entered into a world that was as old as cedar and water. It was almost a different plane of existence, and we all felt the change. Our focus evolved and shifted, turning into a traditional way of perception. Everything that we did, the way we thought, was related to the big group, our family, that we travelled with, the Washington State canoes. We were acutely aware of the tides, ▶

Facing page: *A thunderbird design is added to the λ̓uinequala with the help of a cardboard template.*

Kwak'wa̱ka̱'wakw chiefs present a canoe filled with gifts to the Heiltsuk people during the Qatuwas Festival.

Facing page: *Sherry Alfred of Alert Bay, B.C., prepares to land in Bella Bella for the Qatuwas Festival.*

where people were, what needed to be done; we were all very aware of the whole movement of that group of canoes. It was a very real spiritual event. The experience was the same, yet different for all of us. The goal was real clear, and the means that we used to get to the end was new and empowering for all of us. For some people it was a turning point. For me it was a fulfillment. It was as though I was meant to be there, I was destined to accomplish that goal. I fit right into the canoe culture, not in a traditional sense of a thousand years ago, but one which was appropriate for 1993. As we had more experience with the Native bands and the different longhouses and all the different people that we met, it became very clear to us all that this was a rebirth, a resurgence, a continuation of a living culture. We were awed by the extreme power that moved with us: it was almost palpable. It was almost like we were enclosed in a protective cover. Like a power was given to us by all the bands with their prayers; all the people we met, all the people who were at home who couldn't be there but said prayers for us gave us that power; you could almost reach out and touch it. All those people that went on that trip will be spending their whole lives trying to get back to that wonderful, spiritual place.

On all the canoe trips we have been on since, I think we have attained a level of reward and a sense of that sacred work that is done for a traditional purpose. There is no school you can go to, no books you can read to learn that. It will continue; it has not stopped. There is a resurgence of the canoe culture for all of the tribes on the Northwest Coast. The canoe is a tool to relearn your own culture, for focussing cultural traditions, because it's like a physical embodiment of age-old cultural teachers. The sacredness of the cedar as a living thing: it stands obedient, then is taken and transformed into another form of teacher. The time given to a canoe journey is a very big sacrifice, but what you do get are some lessons on how to live your life, be centred, how you fit into your tribe, your community, as well as how others around you fit into your community. It's a great gift to be able to learn from the cedar tree that you do matter, that you do count. We've gone on several canoe trips since Bella Bella, and the canoe becomes someone you know and miss; you think of it when you're not around and hold it in very high regard. Once this canoe way of knowledge is found the journey is over and the enjoyment of life begins.

Facing page: *A paddle, used for many hours on the water, becomes an extension of the puller. Often a puller will carve and paint his or her own paddle prior to the journey.*

FRED PETERS

DITIDAHT

Nitinat Lake, B.C. Born 1938

I built a fifty-two-foot canoe for the Sooke Nation. It was from a very big log they felled in Williams Creek in the San Juan Valley. This is pretty well the last of the really big timber that was in there. There's not too much big timber around any more; you got to go a long ways into the woods to get it now. I learned from my dad. He was a well-known canoe builder on the coast. His name was Kelly Peters. He learned to carve canoes from his dad, that was the tradition. He built all his own canoes. He used to gill-net with them, with a roller on the back, on the Nitinat Lake, which used to be open for sockeye. He'd make a new canoe every season, and after the season he'd sell it. I built my first canoe when I was fourteen years old. My dad helped with it a lot, straightened it all out after I got it shaped out.

There hasn't been many canoes around for years. This canoe I built at Sooke is the first big one in seventy to eighty years. Canoes are starting to come back because culture is coming back in most Native nations up and down the North American coast.

I cut out the bow with the power saw, then I plane the bottom out smooth. Get everything right level before I even start shaping it. The bottom, the level, has to be right on. I put the level to it and get the bottom flat and straight, then I start shaping it. I cut it into a wedge shape, and I put a point at both ends and I work it from there. Then there's not much to shaping the bottom. It's hard to see where you're going with a log that big, but a lot of it is imagination, you see it before it's even done. It's shaped on the bow more than anything else. You need to have a good slope on the top of the gunwales, so when you look at it from the front it's got a good flow. I take all the corners off next, and I leave the middle alone, because that shapes out itself. I use power tools now, but my dad used all hand tools: an adze, axe and hand plane. I seen him make a twenty-five footer, take him a month and a half. I made that big one in four months. He used to do eighteen- to twenty-footers in three to four weeks before fishing started. He'd shape the inside with an axe, a plain double-bladed axe. Now I use a power planer and sand the inside and outside. I have a knife, called a draw knife, that I use, then I sand the rest to get out the slivers. To hollow it, we chunked a solid thirty-foot piece out with a power saw. With that piece I can still make another thirty-foot canoe. The bow I added on later. ▶

Previous page: David Neel's twenty-five-foot canoe: shaped, hollowed out
and ready to be steamed.

*Pegs of a premeasured length, called finding pegs, help the carver to achieve the correct thickness
for the canoe's sides and bottom.*

Mark Henderson, Weiwaikum, uses marine enamel paint to put a thunderbird on the side of the k̓ʷuinequala.

I think this revival of canoes is going to continue. I have a contract to go to Bamfield to make another canoe, as big as the one I just finished at Sooke. There'll be more travel by canoe now, for ceremonial things. The guys who worked with me on the Sooke canoe, they didn't learn enough yet. But I'm going back because there's three more to do there. They're going for a forty-eight-foot racing canoe. I figure it takes about three canoes before a guy catches on. If I left them alone on the second one it wouldn't be as good as the first one. I have to be right with them to do it. Like my dad—he was there every day to straighten out any mistakes I made. Then he'd put a mark for me to follow and I didn't go beyond that line. I've seen the tradition come and go in my lifetime; it's good to see it come back.

HENRY ROBERTSON
KEMANO-KITLOPE
Vancouver, B.C. Born 1934

I became involved with the canoe expedition to Bella Bella when the young fellas asked me in Vancouver. Gary Wilson, Gerald Stewart and Oscar Swanson came to my place, brought me half a salmon, which is the traditional thing to do when you are going to ask a favour of a chief. Oscar Swanson asked me if I could guide them as skipper, elder and chief to Bella Bella. I accepted.

I think the canoe is important, really important. It's what our ancestors did. We left Vancouver with nothing, not even a VHF radio. No support boat, nothing. We packed our own groceries and camping equipment. We had no compass or money. We were on our own. Our ancestors, they left home with nothing too. I remember my father telling me he used to paddle with his mother and father out to the steam boats at MacKay Reach to go look for work, go to town. The canoe would be pulled right up onto the deck of the steam boat. From there they would travel to Campbell River or to Vancouver to sell furs. If the prices were too low in Vancouver, they would paddle to Seattle, Tacoma or La Push. From Tacoma they would sometimes go to Idaho to pick hops. They would hide their canoe beside the railroad tracks until they got back.

I paddled canoes when I was young, in the early forties. I would travel with my aunt, Josephine Hall, her husband, Sam Hall, and their son, Max. Sam Hall made Max and me our own paddles. On the river, Kitlope River, Kitlope Lake, there were lots of canoes.

Overleaf: *Crews beach their canoes at Pauquachin, B.C.*

GERALD STEWART
TSIMSHIAN
Richmond, B.C. Born 1964

I got interested in traditional canoes during the Rediscovery Conference in 1992. That was a catalyst to get the kids more interested in their own culture, as I interpret it. For our people the canoe was basically an analogy for what a tribe was, and the water was life. How it paddled during rough waters and such was relevant. The whole canoe is much like your tribe. When someone makes gestures or movements they are noticed by all, and affect the whole group. Things like that aren't relevant these days. We don't exist that way; we're all autonomous individuals. We don't live together, and are not affected by one another in the same way.

I believe in that metaphor and what it says. It's a strong metaphor, the canoe, and has been used by our people for years as they explain and talk to the tribes—in old ways, traditional ways. Tsimshian people who educated me talked about the tribe and referred to it as a canoe. Every move that you make, even though you don't know it, affects all of us.

I started to learn more, speaking to the elders, and the words they choose, the way they say things is so elegant. There are some elders around who know a lot of things. Sometimes if you conduct yourself the right way they'll show you things and educate you. If you don't act accordingly they try to see when you'll be ready. It's all up to you, basically.

I think the journey to Qatuwas was really a catalyst. It gave the people of all these different nations the opportunity to make canoes, and once they have them they won't just leave them sitting idle. In years to come I think we'll see a lot more of this tradition. We were a group that, with the help of Bill Reid, followed through. We moved into the longhouse at U.B.C., used his canoe, *LooTaas,* and he also offered us his twenty-seven-foot dugout. We approached him traditionally, had someone speak for us, tell him who our head man was, Henry Robertson, from the Kemano-Kitlope Nation. We approached him on those grounds, told him what we intended to do and asked his assistance. Asked him if it was possible to use his fiberglass replica of the original *LooTaas.*

Relationships between Native cultures are being bridged by this gathering of canoes. These things haven't really been approached since feasting was outlawed in 1884. So our structure has been destroyed, our international affairs between nations. This canoe gathering can accommodate things like that. I think what we should try to do is bond together and try to address ourselves as a united body with common needs. We're grouped together by non-Native people anyway. If we can do that, it will save us a lot of time with things like land claims.

TOM JACKSON
QUILEUTE
La Push, Washington Born 1947

I've been involved in this canoe rebirth pretty much from the start. We started working with our kids in 1986 to be prepared for the Paddle to Seattle in 1989. I got involved by bringing the children to camps, bringing them on hikes. They hiked eight miles up and down hills, and things like that, in storms, too. They camped in storms, like survival training.

The 1993 trip to and from Bella Bella in two months' travelling really joined the group together. We made a lot of sacrifices for that trip. We took a lot of sacrifices money-wise, which really didn't matter to us at that time, because we had young people involved trying to find themselves, trying to keep away from the drugs and alcohol. All the trips we go on, we stress drug- and alcohol-free. No matter where we go, we try to stress that, because we believe it's important. Myself, I'm an alcoholic, and I haven't used the alcohol for quite a few years, since 1980. And I've been really happy doing what I'm doing, helping the young people. My whole family is culturally aware, making things: paddles, masks, regalia and so on. All the things that we need to prepare for all these trips. My son's a carver and he makes paddles. When he was going to school his class made their first river canoe. Our canoes are very active in our community.

The canoe we use was built in 1928, and it was like a challenge that we had within ourselves to rebuild it and use it. "Can we have it ready for the paddle?" we asked. The people that gave it back didn't take care of the canoe. It was all rotted in different spots. We had to do a lot of cutting out and putting new pieces in, then we cleaned the whole canoe from one end to the other. It took us nine months to refurbish this canoe, which is harder than making a canoe. When you get in it you can feel something different about it. We had the canoe blessed in our way, with the cedar boughs and songs. We gave it a name, gave a party for the canoe and our elders. We named the canoe *Kowea,* which means "Steelhead," because the steelhead travel in the waters, they always ▸

69

Calvin Hunt, Kwakwa̱ka̱'wakw, uses an elbow adze to hollow out the I-Hos, *the Comox Nation's canoe. The straight sides of the canoe will be steamed into graceful arcs, adding a foot to the width.*

go out to sea and they always come back. We have other canoes at home but this is the one we've been using because it's a smaller, ocean-going canoe. It doesn't take too much to move it, the young people to enjoy it. We've been in quite a few storms. We were really safe with our canoe.

The spirituality plays an important role in the canoe, especially when you start feeling down, the fellows start feeling bummed out. Then you start singing. Then you sing your paddle song, then the canoe moves. Then everything goes real good. Then we put up the sail; the sail plays a great deal in this too, we have our sail blessed too. I see the canoe movement continuing to grow.

SAM WOSS
HAISLA
Kitimat, B.C. Born 1910

ROBERT STEWART
HAISLA
Kitimat, B.C. Born 1942

Sam: I worked on canoes before, done lots of orders. In my days, they never used to teach you how to build a canoe. You got to be there to watch them. I was glad I took it up and learned from one of the old masters, Tom Nyce Sr. I built my own canoe too when I was eighteen. Everybody had to build their own canoe. There was lots of them then. I never did see the war canoes, though.

We don't make the really big canoes, because we use canoes on the river. Use them for oolichan fishing. Some of them were thirty to thirty-two feet. They're easy to handle on the river; that's why they make them small.

This log we used for our canoe is about four hundred to four hundred and fifty years old. This canoe is forty-two feet, seven inches. It was forty-two feet, eight inches but we lost an inch after we steamed it. Steaming pulls it upwards at the bow and stern. Steaming is quite a trick; that's another trade in itself. You got to be real careful. You can crack the canoe, not doing it the right way. It took us over nine hours to steam this canoe.

You take logs and pile it up like a log cabin, and keep piling it, and keep piling rocks. You light the fire and let it burn down, and when the rocks are red hot you put them in the canoe one by one. You put it them slowly, otherwise it'll bust. You got about eight inches of water in the canoe. Gradually it gets hot. You keep adding a few rocks until it starts steaming, then you can put all the rocks in. Cover it with canvas to keep the steam in. Then you start testing it. When the sides start getting soft, you put sticks in to widen it. You keep putting wider sticks in, all along the canoe. ▸

71

The Weiwaikum and Wewaikai people sing their canoe song at the Kwakwaka̱'wakw village of Fort Rupert, B.C.

You cut sticks to size as you do it. You keep it covered up until it's ready to spread. You can see when it's ready to spread. You keep splashing hot water on the sides where it's not moving. The wood becomes very flexible. Sometimes, when you steam it the right way, when the canoe is the right shape, it can spread by itself, without touching it. Then you let it cool and it's finished. When you cool it off you have to spring it back about two inches or it'll split. When it's starting to cool off you spring it back gradually. Our canoe, it sprung back an inch and a half.

Canoe building, it has to be passed on, you have to learn it. We're gonna keep on with this tradition. A lot of the younger generation helped along with the people that built the canoes. I think it really opened their eyes and ears, what's going on with this canoe gathering.

Robert: We built this canoe together. Sam is the teacher. We're one of the few ones that still have an elder, an old master to advise us how to carve. It took us four months, February 15 to June 15, to finish this canoe. It was all done with community work, which is hard to do these days. This is the first time in Haisla history that this has been done with community work.

They used to go down to the United States in those old canoes. I used to hear a lot of old people talking about Seattle, Tacoma, White River and all those places farther down. We can still build canoes today, as good as the old people. We use the axe, the adze; we never really lost that knowledge. I'm quite fortunate that I still have my uncle Sam here to pass on the knowledge that he's got.

MAURICE NAHANEE
SQUAMISH
North Vancouver, B.C. Born 1956

My involvement with canoes started when I was doing the *Rez*, a Native youth magazine. As I was travelling across the country, I met people who were involved with their culture, and I realized I didn't really know about my own. At the time I couldn't sing a song or share a legend with them. And I realized my own kids were getting older, and I wanted to be able to pass my culture on to them. Bob Baker told me about his plans to build a canoe and travel to Bella Bella. I thought, "What a perfect opportunity to learn about my culture." Originally I was just going to be one of the organizers and help the Squamish participate. This was in 1991, and I started working with the ▸

North Vancouver Canoe Club. I wanted to help bring about a revival of our culture and work with the youth. Through helping the canoe club I learned to pull canoe, and about my culture, so I can pass it on to my children.

I actually ended up leaving my job from January to June 1993 to help organize for the journey. We had to do a lot of public awareness to get together a team. Bobby Baker started to put together a team based on their expertise: Richard Baker for his spiritual and team building, Gordon Newman for his canoe-pulling experience, Ian Campbell for his singing and speaking the Squamish language. So on our canoe team we had a lot of specialized personnel. Everybody made an important contribution, but those were some of the key people.

We underwent a lot of physical training, which included running and paddling in the canoe. In the area of spirituality we underwent cold-water baths, which is the traditional Squamish way for spiritual cleansing and healing. We used the sweatlodge for cleansing and to help pull together the team. We participated in vision quests at the hot springs at Mount Baker. It's really important to be a team, and our goal was to be like a family in the way we care for each other.

I was gone for a month on the paddle. It was a long time, and it was hard to be away from my family. I returned to North Vancouver for my daughter Marissa's birthday on July 1, 1993. It was a long time to be away, but then again it was not long enough. Surviving the training was the hardest part, and having the mental ability to stick through it. At the end of the day when we attended a banquet by the host, it was hard to have a good attitude and do your best every time. Above all else, we wanted to give our best presentation to our hosts for the honour they did us in welcoming our team to their community. One of the highlights for me was the feast given at Clam Beach by the Oweekeno people. It was as though time was at a standstill, like the way our ancestors came together. It was a big gathering of all the canoe teams, and the place was so special.

The revival of our songs and maritime traditions is now being used more and more in our communities. We are using the things we learned almost every week. We just had a land claim treaty signing and we used our own songs to greet the chiefs, which hadn't been done in a long time. So we are using the protocol that we learned on the canoe journey. I believe now that the canoe has its own spirit, its own entity. It is like a member of our community.

Facing page: *Chief Danny Henderson, Weiwaikum Nation, awaits his turn to ask Heiltsuk chiefs for permission to come ashore at Bella Bella, B.C.*

JAKE JONES

PORT GAMBLE

Kingston, Washington Born 1936

We done a little canoe, a sixteen-footer, just to learn how to use the adzes and the axes and all the tools we needed to do a big one. The big canoe took us a little over three months. We were in a hurry, so we worked twelve hours a day, six or seven days a week just to get it done. It was three and a half foot wide to begin with, and we steamed it pretty close to five feet across.

The figure carved into the prow is a wolf. Only our tribe, from Puget Sound, has that design. There was a couple of old canoes in our area, and we went up and took the measurements off of them. We took all those dimensions and brought them back and designed our canoe from that. We had a thirty-five-foot log so that's what we had to go by. Our canoe is pretty close to two inches thick in the bottom, and about seven-eighths of an inch in the sides.

We drilled a hole and placed a peg every two feet. When you hollow out down to the drill hole, you know you're getting close to the thickness you want.

We have been using our canoe for ceremonies, and we've been teaching our young people how to paddle, how to use the canoe. We had to build it and have it done for the Paddle to Seattle. Everybody thought we couldn't do it, but we done it. It was a really good thing for our tribe, because we haven't had canoes since the 1800s. We've brought the canoe back. Now we have this canoe, a sixteen-footer and a racing canoe, so we're going to get the youth involved, for races and that. I think bringing the canoe back can help more people hang on to their culture. It really helps you when you go out and paddle a canoe; no matter if you're old or young, it is real good therapy when you're paddling. You get the feeling of being on the water with your stroke kind of working together, with the youths, elders and everybody; it brings us closer together. It was hard to get people interested in paddling. You would think there would be people lining up to do it, but there weren't. We needed at least twenty-two paddlers to go to Bella Bella, so we could run two shifts all the time. There is ten paddlers and one guy to steer.

Every place we go there is always people taking pictures of our canoe and asking us about it. We explain about our tribe, how we built it and what the canoe is all about. We find this of interest to Native and non-Native people both.

Facing page: *The Squamish canoe,* K̲xwu7lh, *at Indian Island, B.C.*

JACK PLANE
SOOKE
Sooke, B.C. Born 1933

When my brother and I were growing up the beaches were full of canoes. We used to paddle around and clam dig, duck hunt, and crab fish and everything in canoes. We grew up in canoes. That stopped about after World War II broke out. People would come and take canoes and put them in their yards; they'd end up in museums, and rotting on the beach. My little duck-hunting canoe went missing off the beach. Somebody found it, a white guy I guess, and he restored it. One day the Lions Club in Sooke was having a parade and I seen my canoe going by in the parade. I said, "Where'd you get this canoe?" They said, "Oh, we found it drifting around and restored it." "Know where it come from," I said. So they gave it to the museum and they left it there. I told them, when you got your own canoe you know it exactly, it's yours.

I've seen the canoe tradition come and go. We wanted to bring it back for the young people. I noticed that with our canoe, before it was finished there wasn't much interest, but towards the end when everybody saw the shape of it and the size of it, then the interest started. Now everybody is really involved. It shows you what it can do. Not only that, you get to visit other villages, see the people and bring our young people around. We're gonna start going to all these different cultural events, and we're gonna build more canoes. I see this as the start of something, bring it back like we used to, our ancestors.

My elder brother here, Frank Plane, he's the hereditary chief. He has the name of our canoe. It was given to him at a big potlatch there, when we all got our names.

Our prow is from a war canoe. The whaling canoe is a little lower because they used to have to harpoon the whale off the bow. But in the war canoe the bow stands up so a guy can hide behind it when they're shooting at him. Each hereditary family has its own design, way of painting the canoe.

We researched how, in the old days, our ancestors had to fight to keep our nation, the Sooke Nation, our beautiful harbour and all of the fish and clams. Many years of history and stories of how they fought for the territory, until the white man come along and polluted it and all. We're losing it that way now. So this canoe is something to bring it back. Those young people, they mean everything, they're our future. The only resource we have left is our young people. Traditions have to be there, because that's the way we were taught from our elders; we gotta hand it down to them. If we don't, we don't have nothing. We're looking to the ones that aren't even born yet. That's the whole idea, and I think it's a good idea.

Canoe nations travelling to the Qatuwas Festival arrive at Alert Bay, B.C.
In the background is the U'Mista Cultural Centre.

With the assistance of Chief Adam Dick of the Kwakwaka'wakw Nation, Bill Henderson, Weiwaikum, places sacred eagle down in the ƛ'quinequala during its launching ceremony.

Facing page: *A young boy helps hold the Comox Nation canoe, the* I-Hos, *in place during a welcoming ceremony at Pauquachin, B.C.*

VICTORIA WELLS

EHATTESAHT

Campbell River, B.C. Born 1964

We commissioned Carl Martin and his brother Joe Martin to do two canoes. We worked with the school from Campbell River. Most of the kids from the Ehattesaht Band went to the Central Elementary School. We wanted to give them an opportunity to see a canoe being built. We set it up as a learning situation for a young carver. Coulson Forest Products donated two logs, which were brought to the school. Mr. Black, the principal, provided us with a carving space. From those logs a twenty-four-foot and a twenty-seven-foot canoe were carved.

Carl and Joe started carving the first canoe in November 1990 and were finished a little before Christmas. Some kids were so disappointed that they used chain saws and other tools. The students would say, "You're not supposed to make canoes like that." They were quite irate. There were a couple of young men who visited with the carvers who told them, "You're not supposed to hollow out a canoe that way; they're supposed to be burned with fire." After the canoes were finished an elder, Lily Michaels, and Earl Smith, my grandfather, decided that they would give them both a name. One is *Hlilt-he-ya-chist,* that's the twenty-seven-foot one, the other is *Hahk-kla-sis.*

One of the things that we wanted to do was create an economic base on the West Coast. Fishing and logging have sort of disappeared; so have a lot of other resource-based jobs. Tourism was another avenue. We wanted to create an education for non-Native people to come and explore, because when you go into a museum you get this museum experience of a Native person being part of the past. All of the teachings about Native people, even in school, are about what they did, what they were, never how we are now. One of the things that we wanted to express is that we're very much alive. Our culture is alive. It hasn't died, it's been in the winter phase. The use of canoes has been in a winter, and it's coming into spring now. We couldn't imagine using a canoe as a full-time way of life any more, but a way of exploring with other people.

One area of use for the canoes is with the school system, creating and expanding the Native curriculum. The principal in Zeballos is really interested in working with the Ehattesaht and Nuu-chah-nulth people to come up with a canoe society that will educate people to rebuild character and self-esteem, like an Outward Bound program.

The Namgis canoe, Ga̱luda, *leads the way into Alert Bay on the journey to Bella Bella.*
The loon carved on the prow has wings that flap.

The Squamish canoe, K̲xwu7lh, leads the great canoes into Pauquachin, B.C., during the Tribal Journeys paddle.

MORRIS WHITE

HAIDA

Masset, B.C. Born 1931

CHRIS WHITE

HAIDA

Masset, B.C. Born 1962

Morris: My father used to be a boat builder, so woodwork comes easy to me. I studied pictures and a few old canoes, but basically we knew about canoe design just like we had a microchip in us. This is old knowledge that is being learned again. Our first canoe, we finished it in 1987. We took it to Hydaburg, Alaska, in 1989.

In building a canoe you have to visualize what it will look like after it's steamed wider, so that makes it a lot more difficult. You have to predict how wide it's going to be, the level of the sides; it's all thought out ahead of time. The steaming also changes the way it moves through the water. The angle of the sides keeps the canoe up on the swells, rather than the swells hitting it straight on. There's a formula. The formula's right in the log, if you look at it carefully.

The canoe has to be taken down stage by stage. When we're going through the first few steps of shaping the canoe we can see from our centre line how much we have to take off, what's going to come out of the log. We try to maximize the amount of wood we're going to keep.

We wanted to learn what our grandfathers had, use this new technology with the old technology. Make the canoe live longer. Old days a canoe used to last fifteen to thirty years. Today we have less manpower and more power tools. It's still a tedious task. We had four or five men to finish three canoes this year.

My sons were interested in boat building, like my father, so we thought we'd get started a few years ago. Our people are losing their sea-going way of life. We're going to take it back as a mode of transportation. I think it's going to keep bringing back a lot of pride to our village.

I know that I'm not going to stop building canoes. The way I see it, it's going to be a mode of transportation for some of the people who want to go back to the old village sites and our fishing camps. There's probably many children in our village that have never been in a boat, let alone a canoe. There's many children who have never seen our islands, and our islands are so beautiful. I've been living here for thirty years and I haven't seen enough of them. My grandfather, Geoffrey White, he took us river fishing for sockeye when I was seventeen and he knew every part of the islands. He knew the rocks, the reefs, the sandbars, the tides, and he taught me a few things. All we had when we were growing up was a small skiff. Mainly I see the canoe as opening up our territory for our people. ▶

Wayne Alfred, Namgis, dances to welcome canoe crews to Alert Bay, B.C.

You have to learn how to paddle. Everyone has to learn how to paddle, work as a team. The main skill is developing balance. The paddlers have to know how to balance and kind of roll with the wave a bit; they learn how to move in the canoe. A lot of times people in power boats get interested so they power up to us, and it seems they are trying to sink us. Everyone gets a little nervous, but after a while we develop faith in the canoe. We know the canoe can handle it.

We have lost quite a few things, not only culturally. During the early part of the century the Haidas built a lot of their own boats. They started off building schooners, schooner fishing boats. When they had power they started building gillnetters, and after that they got into seiners. They had quite a fleet. In those days they were quite good fishermen and they fished along the whole coast. All of a sudden that was taken away from them with some fancy pen work from the companies, and our people in Masset were left with no industry except for a few cannery workers and loggers. People started turning back to carving again. In the early 1960s it was an older generation of carvers.

Chris: My dad came up with the idea of building the canoe twenty-something years ago. He was looking way ahead. I never heard about it until he actually had the logs delivered and we started working on our canoe. For this trip we had a lot of young carvers. We had them make their own paddles. That made them feel proud, to be paddling using their own paddle.

My dad is never satisfied until it's perfect. He has an eye, because he's worked on boats before. Every step of the way it's slow, but I know we can't rush because we might make a mistake. Every canoe is different. You can use a formula to a certain point, but every log has its characteristics.

Gordon Newman, Squamish, relaxes while waiting for the tide to change.

MERVYN CHILD
KWAKWA̱KA̱'WAKW
Fort Rupert, B.C. Born 1955

My first involvement in the canoe story was in preparation for the Qatuwas Festival. Calvin Hunt and I went to Victoria and studied some old canoes. He also got some information from a friend, and away we went. We left our canoe really thick at first but have become more confident and lightened it since.

The way the hull changed when we spread it was fascinating. The real education came after the canoe was complete. It demands that you work together; the canoe is only as comfortable as its crew. I cannot think of a better tool for working with a group.

I didn't appreciate the power of a canoe song until I sang one while canoeing. It teaches you to breathe, gives you rhythm and sets the pace. I have since that voyage learned a great deal, and I have respect for those who demonstrate proper canoe etiquette and share the canoe way of learning. To all of them I am grateful. *Gala Kasla.*

CALVIN HUNT
KWAKWA̱KA̱'WAKW
T'sakis (Fort Rupert), B.C. Born 1956

The *I-Hos,* Comox First Nation's canoe, is our second canoe. The first was the canoe we carved in Fort Rupert. We named that canoe *Maxwalogwa* after my mother, Emma Hunt.

Mervyn Child, my nephew, instigated the carving of our first canoe. We felt that the Kwagiutl of Fort Rupert should be represented in the Qatuwas gathering in Bella Bella. Eugene Arima, a good friend, provided us with valuable information in the form of plans for a thirty-two-foot canoe. Mervyn and I did some research at the Royal B.C. Museum. We photographed canoes and made drawings and templates against the lines of various canoes.

The learning process in canoe building brought people together, helped us to work with one another and taught us the richness of our culture. Canoe building indirectly has helped in the revival of our traditions of the past.

*Jeff Edwards, Coast Salish,
acts as honour guard during the
Parade of Nations, part of the
Commonwealth Games First Nations
celebrations in Victoria, B.C.*

CONRAD WILLIAMS
PENELAQUAT
Queets, Washington Born 1947

BILL JOHNSON
MAKAH
Neah Bay, Washington Born 1942

The canoe is a lot more than a boat. It's what the tree gave. Everything runs in a parallel purpose. Everything in this world has a soul. In our language (Makah) Cha-bot is God. Cha-bot made it, he gave it a soul. Before the beginning of time he was still putting the world together. He gave the rocks a soul. There are Indian doctors, what today we would call medicine men, who know how to use the soul of the rock. We've heard of these, we believe in them. Like these young kids who crossed the Juan De Fuca Strait in our canoe. They didn't believe until we were halfway across that we could make it. Belief is half the battle, belief in anything you want. You have to have belief in the Creator first because he'll help you, then you help yourself, and the fellas you're with.

There's a spiritual side to canoeing, to everything. Everything has a life, everything has a spirit, and everything has a path. That log was meant to be a canoe, other parts of it, the roots, were meant to be baskets, the bark was meant to be used for clothing. These things take on another life.

We were on a quest, a quest to open up to nations up here who haven't talked to each other for many years. Even a war could not have brought people together the way canoes have.

BILL WASDEN
NAMGIS
Alert Bay, B.C. Born 1944

When Frank Brown came to Alert Bay for the elders' conference in 1990 I opened my big mouth and made a promise to Frank that I would arrive in Bella Bella in 1993 with a canoe. Of course when I got my senses together I didn't have a canoe, didn't know anyone who knew how to build one and didn't have the wherewithal to build one myself. So that's how it all started. Well, we got a hold of Dick Dawson and he'd built a few canoes for display. We did a lot of research in the provincial museum in Victoria; we had a lot of arguments. I think the basis of carving a canoe is that we let the log tell us what to do with it. Sometimes we would let it sit for days and just look at it, and eventually it would come to you as to what to do with that log. ▸

Pullers help to launch the K̲xwu7lh, *the Squamish Nation's canoe. Bill Reid's* LooPlex *is in the foreground.*

Canoes prepare to come ashore at Pauquachin, B.C.

Facing page: *Ronnie McKinny, in bear mask, and Simon Wallace, in thunderbird headdress, dance in the bow of the Namgis canoe, Ga̱luda.*

The canoe is so very important to our culture. It seems to be a healing tool, especially for the youth. When they come into the canoe, their attitudes change and their respect for their culture, and they conduct themselves with dignity when they're in the canoe. There's a healing aspect for anybody that goes into that canoe. For everybody, especially on these long journeys, you learn so much about yourself and other people. You learn the respect and the ability to work as a team, and you always have to rely on somebody else to carry you through. No one individual can do it themselves. Teamwork is an important part.

I think in our modern world the canoe is going to lead the way. It's bringing our youth back to our culture. It's teaching them the disciplines our forefathers knew.

LAURA HOWELL
COMOX
Cumberland, B.C. Born 1968

The Comox Band had the opportunity to host the canoes from the south as they came through to Bella Bella in 1993. It was really inspirational for our community. Before, it was really hard to get the community together, but the whole group came together to support the canoes from the south. It was then we thought, "Hey, we could have our own canoe." We made friendships with people outside the community who were very encouraging; they offered skills on how to get going. We found a lot of support among our own people as well. The next step was where to get a log. We managed to get our log, a cedar about four hundred years old, donated by MacMillan Bloedel from Kelsey Bay. We got a forty-one-foot log, from which we got a thirty-two-foot canoe and two small totem poles. We had Calvin Hunt and Mervyn Child carve our canoe. The funding came from a lot of sources: selling T-shirts and caps, donations, a salmon barbeque and raffles.

Previous page: The K̲xwu7lh, canoe of the Squamish Nation, is carried to the ocean with the help of many strong hands.

When we had the launch it was a real public event. We gave rides to the public. It was only a few weeks before the Paddle to Victoria when we got our canoe in the water. Before that we were practising in a regular factory-made, six-man canoe. It's been about eighty years since the community's been involved in canoes. We wanted to get one again when we realized how important the canoe was to our ancestors. It brings back other parts of the culture as well: the singing, dancing and feasting. It brings the community together. With the drumming comes the drum-making and other parts of the traditon. It's sort of a tool for the community. All the people respected the canoe as more than a boat. We called it *I-Hos,* which means "Sea Serpent" in our language. The paddlers spoke of it like a living thing.

We found we had to learn to paddle with each other, learn to respect each other in the canoe. We knew that we would have to spend a lot of time together, and we practised three or four times a week so we could get used to each other. We had to leave anything bad on the shore, learn to work together. As the time to make the trip came closer people got more spiritual, more motivated and more energized. More interested in getting involved in the planning, not letting someone else do it for them. They had their own vision of what travelling in the canoe was going to be, and they wanted to make it happen.

We're still paddling now, trying to get the kids out. We definitely plan to make more trips. We have relatives in Powell River and Sechelt, we'll go visit there. We go on day trips to Tree Island, where our ancestors used to go. There's going to be big trips every summer now. About fifty of our people went on the Paddle to Victoria. That's quite a few when we have only about 140 band members living on reserve. I think it brings all the communities together, not just our own, the other Kwakwaka'wakw nations as well. I remember when we came into a Salish village one of their chiefs said, "This is the first time that canoes from the northern tribes came in peace into Salish territory."

The Elwha S'Klallam canoe, Warrior, *arriving at Clam Beach in Oweekeno (Rivers Inlet) territory on its way to Bella Bella, B.C.*

WILLY HUNT
KWAKWAKA'WAKW
Fort Rupert, B.C. Born 1906

When I was young they'd go all the way to Vancouver in canoe. There was lots of canoe in Fort Rupert, that's all they use before I was born. They were still around when I was young. They used to be tough guys when they make the canoes, no power saw, just the axe and stone. They make the canoe in the bush, maybe twenty young fellas to bring it down, pull it out. When they make that Edward Curtis film *In the Land of the War Canoes,* my dad was there. They had a bear dancing in the bow, eagle too; they really did that in the old days. Canoe, that all my dad use when he went to Alert Bay and potlatch. When they come home, my uncle was in the canoe, big wind and the canoe cracked, with the sails, hey, all drowned, twenty-two, all Kwakwaka'wakw. Had a cloth sail, canoe cracked in big wind, all drowned. That's what they say.

They used to give away canoes in potlatch. One time, Spruce Martin, he cover maybe half a dozen canoe with boards, give away. There at Alert Bay, on the point, we call it Kum-gia, he good *hamatsa.* Lots of them give away that time. Used to give away lots of canoes, old days. Lots of canoes when I was young, the whole village. These young people they never see the canoe before.

FERMIN SANCHEZ
SHOSHONE/BANNOCK
La Push, Washington Born 1962

I'm always interested in supporting the people. I'm a Plains Indian, from Idaho, and I'm a Sun Dancer, and a member of the American Indian Movement. Our whole lives have been dedicated to helping Indian people one way or another. I own a fishing vessel and I live in La Push, Washington, and they asked me to act as support boat for the canoes. There was a lot of reasons why I should go and shouldn't go. The reasons I shouldn't go all involved money, because I am in the business of fishing. Really, that wasn't a good enough reason not to go on this trip. Of course I'm in the business to make money, that's what we do. But they didn't have a support vessel, and I couldn't see myself making money while those people were in danger. I'm trained with the sea ▸

for a lot of years, so I knew I could be some good help to them. Originally I started out as support boat for one canoe and ended up as support boat for four canoes.

Our culture is the most important thing in our life. I see this here as the big salmon, the big salmon that came from the Haida, came from the Quileute, came from the Suquamish. It came from all these tribes to Bella Bella to spawn. Then it's gonna go home and it's gonna spawn more canoe expeditions and more of these traditional ways. Our traditional ways are the foundation of life for Indian people; it's the one thing we have that we can grasp. They've taken everything else. They've taken all this land, they've taken everything away from us, and attempted to destroy the culture with alcohol and drugs and this type of thing. This culture we have is our strongest asset. It's gonna continue to make the people strong. These young people that I've seen singing and dancing here, it's gonna make them feel proud and it's gonna make them teach their kids. And it's gonna be a continuation. As I see it, without this culuture and this way we're doomed. Because it's the centre of our life. It's the land, the culture, the elders, the children, those are the things that make us different and unique as a people.

ETHEL ALFRED
NAMGIS
Alert Bay, B.C. Born 1910

There was lots of canoes when I was small. They used to have lots of canoes on the beaches and there was some really huge ones that I seen. They had carvings on the bow. That's how they travelled, eh? The canoes were used when they had potlatches in other villages. Different tribes came in their own canoes and they would dance as they were going into the village that invited them. I know my cousin used to do that, he'd be dancing on the bow of the canoe, the peace dance. Some were *Tsexa K'sala* and then you had to give money out to the people that were around when you got into the village. Some dancers had masks like the bear, and they used to come and dance on a board set up across the canoes.

They used to travel all the way from Victoria to Village Island by canoe. I don't know how they did it; the trip would be a week or so anyway. They must have been very good paddlers then. I remember my friend used to tell us about when the village was burned, all the bighouses were burned while they were in Victoria. A child had died, and they had to go and bring the body by canoe back to Village Island. The bighouses were still smoking when they got there.

Our people quit using the canoe right around the turn of the century. The people started using small gas boats instead of canoes for fishing. I guess the canoes are coming back because the younger generation wants to learn about our ways. In my lifetime, I've seen them go and seen them come back.

I think it's very good to see the canoes return. It makes me feel good that the young people want to learn the ways of our ancestors. But I don't think we can be the same, really. Things were different in the early years. People acted different and the things they did; the way the kids are today it has really changed. The more I think about it, it has really changed.

BILL HELIN
TSIMSHIAN
Parksville, B.C. Born 1960

This canoe, a forty-foot vessel that will accommodate twelve to fourteen paddlers, it's kind of the last educational process for me as a native artist. I've experimented with every other realm of woodcarving and now this, to me, is kind of like a full circle. Coming back to the way I started my career as a fisherman, then got injured to the point where I couldn't do anything but rehabilitate as an artist. It's taken me in this direction. The more I got into it the more I realized the passion in it and how much more exciting it is than doing any other artform that I've been challenged with.

In building a canoe, we're passing on a life form from the forest and reshaping it so that we can transport ouselves in it. It will be a vessel of aesthetics, as well as being functional. It has so much more use than any other piece of artwork. In canoe building, every step of the way you're wondering if this is going to work, and how it's going to work. I think that's the glory of working on this kind of project. Once you get the log in the ocean, what's it going to do? We're taking this tree that was close to the end of its life and carrying that life along. I'll always envision this beautiful cedar tree out in the forest and it had its destiny, and its destiny was to be part of history. It's got a life, it's got a character all its own, once it's all painted up and sitting pretty in the water as *Raven Song*.

The carving of this canoe has brought in the community quite a bit. We've got a canoe committee started, people have actually wanted to raise money to have the canoe stay in the area. ▶

It will end up on permanent display in the new Qualicum Beach recreation facilities. It will be hung from the ceiling above the swimming pool. *Raven Song* is a northern-style Tshimshian canoe, the first from our village in over twenty-five years.

Carving a canoe, it's a labour of love and a passion, once your vision is to be pulling with the other pullers and standing on the bow, pounding the drum like crazy, watching those waves break on your streamlined vessel. It's the idea that you're going to join up with pullers from other areas of the coast, unified in a historical event, to paddle down the coast with other canoes.

DR. GEORGE LOUIE
NUU-CHAH-NULTH
Victoria, B.C. Born 1912

I made my first canoe in the 1930s, helping out my dad. The side walls of a canoe should be about two fingers thick, not too thick or it won't steam right. The bottom should be about three fingers thick. When you stand at the stern or bow and look down the sides you can tell where it is thick by looking. When the canoe is finished you have to be careful when you're setting it down; don't drop it or it will crack. If it does crack, and it's a clean crack, you drill a hole there on both ends so it won't split any further. Then you can make what they call a butterfly joint to hold the crack together, put one about every eighteen inches, then use white-man glue to hold it. Canoes tend to crack a lot right where the centre of the log is.

When you start your log you take what was the north side of the tree and that will be the bottom, that's what we do. There's usually more branches on the south side because it gets more sunshine. You have to be very careful looking at the rings; that will tell you which side should be the bottom. You don't want your canoe too thick because it will tend to crack. Three fingers thick in the bottom; for a smaller canoe, say eighteen feet long, it's only two fingers thick.

Sometimes you got to repair a bad piece of wood. After you cut out the bad section, you replace it with a piece which has all round corners, no sharp corners; it's stronger that way. When you're trying to fit it, you paste the edge with ashes, and when you fit the piece onto the canoe you tap it with a hammer, then you can see where it needs to be trimmed down. Then you drill and peg the new piece of wood to make it strong. You cut a groove into the end of each peg and fit a little ▸

Old-growth Western red cedars are preferred for canoe building. This log, which became the Weiwaikum Nation canoe ƛ'uinequala, was more than eight hundred years old.

wedge in, so that when you tap it into the hole you've drilled the wedge hits the end and spreads the peg so that it won't come out of the hole. It can take a couple of days to fit a piece of wood into a canoe properly.

I built a big canoe in Denmark, forty-two feet long. The log was just about six feet wide at the butt end when I started. There wasn't even a knot in that whole log! I built another canoe, twenty-two feet long; it went to the Ontario Science Centre.

I liked to watch my grand-uncle, two of my uncles and my father and my mother carve canoes. Carving a canoe, it's hard the first couple of days, but after you're out there every morning it gets better.

LIZ McLEOD
BAND MANAGER, COMOX NATION
Courtenay, B.C. Born 1953

The Bella Bella festival got our community interested in having our own canoe. That year when the canoes came through, several of our young people went with them to Campbell River. And some followed the canoes to Bella Bella. They came back really wanting to participate in this sort of thing. The year of the Commonwealth Games seemed to be the year to join in. I think it's very important for the young people, actually for our entire community, to have our own canoe. Even the older people that have come along have experienced a real wish to get back into their culture and to join in.

I think the canoe is the central part of the process to bring everyone together. I know the night our canoe went into the water, I had tears in my eyes and so did everyone else. It was such a beautiful thing. We're already talking about doing a journey to an adjoining village. Everybody wants to keep the canoe in the water and keep it going.

I think the canoe has a place today; it's a way of people getting themselves closer together. It forms a community around that canoe, and everybody has a part of it.

Simon Wallace, of the Namgis canoe, in a thunderbird headdress.

HENRY GEORGE
GWA'SALA'NAKWAXDA'XW
Port Hardy, B.C. Born 1938

This was the first canoe we built for our village. Dick Dawson was head carver. I wanted to do that canoe because I thought of all my old people who were good carvers; all that time I was working I thought of them. We built that canoe in twenty-two days from start to finish, twenty-eight feet long. It would hold ten paddlers and the steersman.

I think it's a real good experience for younger people to know how the old people got around, and how fast they could go. We figured our canoe goes a good ten knots anyway, sometimes twelve. It really brought our people together, but I guess the best thing that we done was form a circle every time, before we touched the canoe. Simon Dick had that smudge; we used that every morning before we started. That's why we didn't feel so exhausted within that twenty-two days, the spiritual help there. The spirituality is really important. We kept telling the people who'd been drinking, when they'd come to visit us while we were working, to come back when they were sober. There is just no way we would even allow them to go near our canoe. You have to have a clear mind to operate the tools. You had to always respect the canoe; that was a big part of it, you had to respect what you were doing, and each other. It gives you a real strong mind, a clear mind, knowing where you're from and who you are as a family. I see a lot of good things from my family. My cousins who worked with us told me that they never saw anything like the way we all worked together without having any hard feelings for each other.

FRANCIS HORNE
COAST SALISH
Duncan, B.C. Born 1954

I've been a carver for about twenty years. Now I'm head carver at the Duncan Native Heritage Centre. This is my first canoe. It was the flotilla of ocean-going canoes travelling to the Commonwealth Games that got me interested. I wanted to take my skills as an artist and use them to advantage on a canoe. I built this canoe with John Bagley and my son, Francis Horne Jr.

Previous page: *The x̱uinequala outside Namu, B.C., en route to Bella Bella.*

There's a big difference between carving a totem pole and carving a canoe. There's such a spiritual vibration with a canoe. When you're doing a vessel for any kind of trip, especially on an ocean, that is just a wild feeling. The very first night I started my canoe, roughing it out, I started having dreams about it. I normally never have dreams about my work. In the dream there were these four old ladies, these four elders, they came to visit me, and they were talking to me in Indian. I didn't know what they were saying, but they were really happy about what was going on. And the next morning when I came in, there was a feather in my canoe. The next day my son came in and he found a feather in the canoe. And it kept happening until there was four feathers. I thought this was unbelievable, so we ended up naming the canoe the *Salish Feather.*

My canoe is forty-two feet long. The tree was about nine hundred years old. There's something special about a piece of wood like that. There's all kinds of things that go through your mind, through your heart. Just imagine the things this tree has seen.

The canoe is a fundamental part of our culture. We always live near water, no matter where: rivers, salt water, lakes. The canoe was all you had between you and the elements. So there was a real craft to building one. How well you gained, how safely you travelled was all on the shoulders of the canoe builder. Restarting tradition is the only thing I'm interested in. My grandfather was a canoe maker. There hasn't been one in the family since he passed away. He was the last hereditary chief of the Tsawout.

AL CHARLES
ELWHA S'KLALLAM
Port Angeles, Washington Born 1972

I became interested in building a canoe in 1989, because of the Paddle to Seattle. Somebody just came up and asked me if I wanted to go and that's where it took off. It was like it opened my eyes to our culture. I was raised to learn our songs and stuff, but never about the canoes and the way it was back in the olden days. That trip just opened my eyes, not just the singing and dancing part but also to the way of our ancestors. It just amazed me. I started out learning about our culture, and once I learned it I ended up becoming a teaching person for our tribe. Now I work with our youth. ▸

Kwakwa̱ka̱'wakw chiefs gather on the beach at Campbell River, B.C., to witness the launching ceremony for the Weiwaikum canoe, ⱡ'uinequala.

Pullers from Washington State prepare to leave from Clam Beach, B.C., on their way to the Qatuwas Festival.

A hok-hok mask, a hamatsa *neck ring and cedar boughs adorn the bow of the Weiwaikum canoe,* ƛ'uinequala, *for the traditional welcome into Bella Bella.*

The log for my canoe was six foot across when I began. We marked the line down the side we wanted, and we split it with some four-foot cherry tree wedges. It took us about three and a half hours. I had an elder helping, to tell me what to do. When it was split it was amazing to hear, you know, like thunder! It was so loud when it snapped, it was so crisp, and you could feel it.

I had a lot of lookie loo's, as the canoe was being built; they would stop by every day and ask me what I was making. After two months I finally asked for some assistance from my tribe. There was no way we could have gotten the canoe ready for Bella Bella with just myself working on it.

When it came time to leave we had to go with it unfinished. It weighed probably about 1,500 pounds. We designed it for eight pullers and the captain. It took us five and a half hours to get from our reserve in Port Angeles to our first stop. We didn't even have the prow or stern pieces added on. We rested up for roughly a week when we got to Cowichan Bay. I've got some relatives up there. This one elder carver, his name is Cicero August, he seen us pulling. He offered to have some of his apprentices come over. So he brought over his crew, and he wouldn't let me do nothing. He said we were in his land, and he was honoured to have us there and to work on our canoe.

When we got to Alert Bay, I figured I would get ahold of some cedar to put on the stern, raise it up. Beau Dick let me in his workshop, gave me a chain saw and an axe and told me he had some cedar down by the water and let me have my pick of it. I went down there and picked a nice chunk and went and put our stern on that day. We pulled into Fort Rupert, and Merv Child, he got a trailer and hauled our canoe from the water to the shop, and then he gave me the pick of his cedar for the bow. When the prow piece was added it looked almost completely new, the shape of it. We're forever in his debt. It wasn't until Nanoose, just outside of Bella Bella, that we totally finished the design of it. Myself and Rick Harry from Squamish, Jake Jones from Port Gamble, a couple other people came out and helped me shape out the bow and finish it. Then we painted it that night. We got done maybe 1:30 A.M., left it on the dock overnight and went to Bella Bella the next day. We were gone two months. Hard to make that kind of time with bills to pay and things.

I think the canoe has a place today. You know, we've had the dugout canoes for hundreds of years; there ain't no way we're going to let go of that. We have the big travel canoes in the water. We've learned a lot. Yeah, a canoe, it's a lot more than just something to sit in and paddle. It's unbelievable, but I talked to our canoe almost every day I carved on it. It's like it can tell when you're out spiritually; it will talk to you.

Squamish paddlers en route to the Qatuwas Festival.

Salish racing canoes in Victoria's inner harbour await the arrival of visiting nations bringing the Queen's Baton to the opening of the 1994 Commonwealth Games.

Al Charles and Margaret Morris in the Elwha S'Klallam canoe, Warrior, *en route to Victoria, B.C.*

RICHARD BAKER

SQUAMISH

North Vancouver, B.C. Born 1951

We're very spiritual people, Squamish people. The teachings of the bighouse are the teachings of the canoe; it's all one entity. Learning to respect one's self, learning to respect the canoe, the value of the canoe, the value of the paddle. The canoe is a vehicle, a return to our traditional pathways. We are exercising our right to travel up and down this coast and share with the people of the world our world, the Indian world. To show them that we're still alive. The gathering of canoes is getting larger and larger, with more awareness of each other's culture, sitting down in circles, bighouses, the teachings.

My grandfather Cecil Brown Sr., who's Haida, he told me, "Once the cedar goes we're no longer Haida." He shared with me the meaning of the cedar; he said, "They're beings just like you and I." That's something I understood very clearly. People have to know more about their own culture and the environment they live in, because it's very important for us to understand that we can't continue to take down the trees.

Everybody represents their beautiful canoe as an extension of their own heritage. Every tree they see now they could see a beautiful canoe, a beautiful totem pole, a beautiful paddle. Someday it's going to be just right to ask the tree's permission to take it down, go through the ceremonies. We have to go out there and tell people that we are the stewards of this land, and not just look at how much a log is worth in dollar signs. We need to be in harmony with the trees because they heal you. Like what's going on here, everybody's discovering who they are, it's a healing process. The young people are getting to understand how to exercise their rights, coming into their own. When they get to their destination, they're going to be very powerful statespeople and spokespersons.

Overleaf: *A throng of Native people in button blankets greet the great canoes as they come ashore at Bella Bella, B.C., for the Qatuwas Festival.*

THE CANOE WAY OF KNOWLEDGE

TOM HEIDLEBAUGH

"It is the cedar canoe that connects us to the old ways."

JOE WASHINGTON

Lummi elder

Ours is a world of cyberspace and television, of shopping malls and suburbs flung to the foot of mountains by the automobile. We imagine this world is made with our will and our science. We travel through it on an information superhighway whose destinations all begin to seem alike.

But there is another world, one of ancient traditions and knowledge drawn from stories told by Raven. This world has been shaped by loving and daring actions, and it is lived in by people who honour their ancestors and work for their families. This world is not bound by time. It is a place where human beings share the watershed with the salmon people and learn the teachings of the cedar tree. Here, feasts can last a week. Potlatches impoverish and enrich in the same instant.

This other world is visited by spirits and guided by prayer. It cannot be approached by airplane or ferry boat or automobile. It embodies a different way of sharing, a different economic and community system, and ultimately a different Way of Knowing. This world can only be reached by the steady stroke of the paddle, the lifted song of the drummer, the carved canoe crossing deep water to be welcomed on the other side by upraised hands.

I first saw the sea-road to this world back in 1970 when I stood on the beach at Neah Bay, Washington, and looked across to the southern tip of Vancouver Island. The Makah elder beside me shook his head. "In the old days we took our great canoes across the strait of Juan de Fuca all the time. We didn't care about the weather. We hunted the whales when they migrated past us. We

Facing page: *Al Charles, Elwha S'Klallam, asks permission to come ashore in the Salish village of Pauquachin, B.C.*

123

got seals in the stormiest seas. We reached for our relatives and gave great feasts. Fifty, one hundred canoes from Ahouset and Ditidaht, from Quileute and Quinault would be lined up on the beach. Time was different back then. We knew things we've forgotten, like the power that lives in the forests. We've forgotten what it was like when the wealthiest man was the one who gave away the most. Nobody went hungry. There were plenty of fish. Now this border separates us and the great canoes are gone. It can never come back, those old days."

I looked across the strait, sharing a bit of the yearning the old man felt. He was remembering a different world from the one in which we stood. Of the scores of ancient canoe styles only the slim, twelve-person racing canoe remained. While we spoke, *Makah I* practised for a race in the harbour. The cedar-and-salmon nations of Canada and the United States still challenged each other in the racing seasons, during festivals like Makah Days or Lummi Stommish, but these modern canoes journeyed to their destinations upended on the welded racks of pickup trucks. The old war canoes, cargo canoes, whaling and sealing and sea-going canoes were long gone, rotting in someone's field, patched up as museum pieces, cut up for firewood: lost.

Those who remembered, up and down the Northwest Coast, hung on to the vision of what the canoe meant. Some carved miniature canoes or exchanged canoe stories at slahel games. Some even "sacrificed" a few cedar logs to relearning the old carving skills. Elders at ceremonies reminded people that the cedar tree was a gift holding a vision within its trunk. With prayer and close attention, traditional carvers had learned to see what waited to come from the cedar log.

When the young men of Bella Bella pulled south to Expo 86, the Vancouver, B.C., world's fair, a barrier was broken. A cultural resurgence began to gather, like a wave once lost in the sea and now building again, restoring itself and picking up energy in "one organic communal act," to quote Heiltsuk leader Frank Brown.

During the Washington State Centennial celebration in July 1989, Hoh and Quileute canoes, carved by traditionalist David Forlines and skippered by him, Fred Eastman, Tom Jackson and others from that whale-hunting nation, went across the deep ocean for the first time in a hundred years. When those three sea-going canoes ended their initial seventeen-hour day by being lifted from the harbour at Neah Bay, another barrier of grief and loss was shattered. The dreams of the elders seemed possible again.

Frank Brown challenged the other nations at Golden Gardens Beach, Seattle, to paddle to Bella Bella in four years' time. The canoe teachings of elders like Nora Barker, Pansy Hudson and Lillian Pullen were realized as people began to live the stories they told. Preparing for the twelve-hundred-mile journey to Qatuwas and back kept us in the ancient vision.

For four years, the Heiltsuk people meticulously constructed a welcome for all who were to come. Frank Brown travelled among the canoe nations, from Haida Gwaii and Nuu-chah-nulth to Elwha S'Klallam and Quileute, working to keep the idea alive. I remember the intense planning sessions he held with Quileute traditionalist David Forlines, who continued to organize in Washington State as his own health declined. Their determination to prepare on the political, spiritual, cultural and personal levels was matched by that of other participants from the S'Klallam and Suquamish communities. At slide presentations and council meetings, the revival of the canoe vision was expressed by many who had gone on the Paddle to Seattle. This new sense of purpose among the Northwest Coast First Nations was epitomized in the testimony of a woman who witnessed the relationship between her own family and the new family of canoes. "Drinking means nothing to my son now. All he wants to do is get in that canoe. He's out on the water, paddling. He wants to carve. He wants to know the cedar." Her body shook with emotion. After each person's powerful testimony we sat silent, in respect of this awareness we were coming to share.

Representatives of the Suquamish and Duwamish people stated they were sharing the responsibilities, costs and purpose of the journey. I remember the extraordinary clarity of Peg Ahvakana's voice as she announced this historic moment of international harmony. When the Lower Elwha, the Jamestown and the Port Gamble tribes formed the S'Klallam flotilla that eventually landed at Bella Bella, unity and healing rose like new wind to old sails.

David Forlines died in 1991, before he could see the canoe gathering his work had encouraged. Before his death, he passed responsibility for his canoe to his close friend Terri Tavenner. Initially the vessel was named *Wads Wad,* after a famous Quileute warrior, then the *Cargo Dog.* For the paddle to Bella Bella, it was known as the *International* canoe because it was shared by so many Northwest and other tribes. David had received extraordinary knowledge from Pansy Hudson and other elders and used it to inspire the canoe resurgence. Working with young people from many U.S. and Canadian tribes over a twenty-year period, David encouraged carving, cedar-bark weaving and understanding of the spiritual roots and stories of the old ways. At his funeral, he was remembered for the traditional wilderness camp he developed with some Shushwap friends at Toleak and for his teachings at the Quileute Tribal School. He was carried to the gravesite in a canoe he had carved. One of the young men he had trained shouted, "David Forlines was one of the greatest carvers!" and we all understood the meaning of that word: a person of knowledge, power, will and art who sacrificed himself to lift up the people through the traditions. A person who saw what lived in the untouched log and released a gift that brought people together as does no other work of tools and human hands.

In the summer of 1993 the long-envisioned gathering became real on the two and a half month journey to Bella Bella and back. We travelled in the old way to Qatuwas, sleeping on the beaches or being welcomed into the bighouses of each nation with feasts and speeches. The *International* canoe carried pullers from Quinault, Queets, Hoh, Quileute, Makah, S'Klallam, Algonquin, Potowatomi, Shushwap, Cape Mudge, Comox and at least ten other nations of canoe peoples as well as non-Native pullers. The years of organizing and preparation were overwhelmed by a deeper reality. When we finally crossed the Juan de Fuca Strait, generations went with us. I doubled as ground crew and paddler on the *International,* and the day of the crossing I stood on the deck of the *Coho,* the Black Ball Ferry from Port Angeles to Victoria. As a crowd of us peered from the steel ship, we caught sight in the distance of the Suquamish Nation's canoe, the *Raven,* and the Elwha S'Klallam *Warrior,* both about an hour's pull away from Victoria's inner harbour. Makah elder and canoe counsellor Mary McQuillen, whose son Scott pulled on the *International* canoe, and Peg Ahvakanah, Suquamish cultural co-ordinator, suddenly broke out their drums and began to sing from the ferry deck. Peg's clear voice cut through the air as if those in the canoes could hear her traditional honour song. The women's drumming took on a special energy that did not end until the canoes were lost from sight.

Peg turned to Mary with tears in her eyes. "Did you see them?"

Mary could only nod, equally moved. They embraced as if completing some great quest. Then Peg turned to those like me who did not have the sight and gently explained, "The ancestors. They were surrounded by the spirit canoes of all the ancestors, leading them across. All the ancient paddlers who crossed in peace for thousands of years were with them." For a moment, looking over the dim water, I could see the mystic flotilla encouraging us on.

Time and again on the journey, many of us gained awareness of this numinous reality, until the demarcation between vision and experience grew less rigid, like a current finding a new path in an old stream. My canoe-mate T. Conrad Williams of Queets received a vision on the hills above Seymour Narrows, and he wore a down-pointing eagle feather until he could deliver his message at Bella Bella.

Elders wept as we brought the canoes in to ancient and accustomed beaches along the way. They saw the raised sails and remembered the family journeys of their youth, when young girls sat in the middle of the canoe weaving baskets as the adults pulled them to feasts or fishing sites. "You are a gift to us," they said. "We never thought we'd see the great canoes again." They told us their stories, gave us their blessings, shook with tears from their wheelchairs or the window seats of pickup trucks driven by their great-grandchildren.

At the Namgis village of 'Yalis, Alert Bay, Kwakwaka'wakw chiefs Frank Nelson and Bill Cranmer stood before hundreds of U.S. and Canadian canoe people in the bighouse and announced the new unity among all the tribes: "Where we once were many nations, fighting among each other, struggling with Canadian and American laws and dealing with the loss of land and fishing and timber rights, now those days are gone. Something has happened with this journey. Where once there were many nations of us, there is now one Canoe Nation." In the silence that followed, I looked around and caught hundreds of nodding heads. The frontiers were shattered, and this amazing energy that we shared was only the beginning of where these carved vessels of healing would take us.

As we travelled in this old way, the modern world became irrelevant. It seemed so much less important than our integration with wind and tide. I heard that in both Suquamish and Kwakwala there were more than twenty-seven words to describe water. The Squamish had fourteen words for different kinds of rain. Exploring these realities became more important than thinking about the jobs and possessions we had left behind. As we camped on uninhabited beaches, sharing songs and cold mush in the rain, we knew that the ancestors had been here before us.

We practised our speeches and discussed protocol. No one wanted to make mistakes that reflected back on their communities, so we prepared carefully to announce ourselves at the old beaches where we were formally welcomed by each nation in turn. Skipper Al Charles Jr., who had carved the Elwha *Warrior*, would stand at the stern and say, "We are the Elwha S'Klallam Nation. In the name of the Creator of all good things, we come in peace. We have travelled a great distance to be with you, to honour your people, to respect your waters and to know this land. We bring greetings from our nations to the south. Like our ancestors, we move carefully on this voyage. We have learned some things and we have come to share with your people so we can learn more. Our hearts are filled with love for you. May we have permission to come ashore?"

From the beach, lined with tribal members, chiefs and elders stepped forward to the water's edge to welcome us. Sometimes a old woman with a quavering voice sang a song possessed by her family that had not been brought out for generations. Somehow she remembered it as we were given permission to turn our canoes and back in to the shore to be feasted.

After we had worked through the dangerous passage of Seymour Narrows, just north of Campbell River, we began to experience the rules behind the canoe teachings. The reasons for the pre-European order of things became apparent, and as we received permission to move north through the waters of each nation, the Canoe Way of Knowledge that sustained the cultures we travelled in became manifest.

A Canoe Way of Knowledge is a bridge between the old ways we yearned for, over long years of suffering, of occupation, disease and disenfranchisement, and the healing hopes of the future. It is a means of understanding the flux of existence. The form and disciplines of a true way of knowing are rare gifts in a time of constant change and uncertainty.

The elders who had come with us, including Mary McQuillen of Makah and Helen Harrison of Quileute, reminded us to be respectful and mindful of every action we made in the northern lands. Each morning was begun with prayer. Each stroke of the paddle was also to be made in prayer, since this was for them a spiritual voyage. It became that to the rest of us as we heard the songs our elders sang to lead us on, sitting in their button blankets in the prow-seat of the canoes.

There was no cursing. Our goal was "no bad thoughts in the canoes." Before we stepped into the canoe each morning, we released any negativity into the cold dawn. We washed anger off the tips of our fingers in the strong, salty water of the sea. We did not carry any feuds or private animosities with us. The whole paddle was alcohol and drug free. We didn't smoke in the canoes. No one was allowed to drop garbage over the gunwales, to urinate, defecate, spit or throw anything into the water in a disrespectful way.

We were made conscious of the canoe graciously bearing us, as a gift from the Creator of the wisdom of the cedar tree. The sea supported us as a responsive blessing to our own attentiveness.

Slowly, as we let the canoe change us, we began to receive experience of the old knowledge. This transforming awareness is perhaps best exemplified by the arrival each morning, as we waited to catch the tide, of an eagle coming from the mountains to the east. It circled our canoes until we all saw it and then shot north to lead us safely through the day.

Sometimes our challenges seemed almost unattainable. We had to become gifts to each other, to the people we visited and to the people who were coming to share in this vision of the Canoe Nation. For this we had to travel in a state of grace, above human anger and human limitations. If we had hostility towards a member of our canoe "family" we were supposed to throw ourselves overboard into the cleansing waters to release our hostility before we could crawl back into the prayer-formed canoe.

I can't remember anyone actually choosing to do this. We were just ordinary folks, laughing and joking, losing our tempers, sulking, forgiving and suffering. Sometimes, when the tension in our canoe grew enormous, Conrad and I became jesters, pitching bad jokes faster then anyone could catch them. We were probably lucky to avoid being thrown overboard, but our humour helped recapture the inspiration that had started us all on our northward path.

Our canoe community grew in size until we were twelve canoes preparing to cross Queen Charlotte Sound in mid-July. We were ready to cross the wide reach of open ocean, to go beyond the protective retreat of calm bays and receptive beaches and make the final run for Bella Bella.

On that morning we held together behind the last island, waiting for a straggling canoe to join us before we surged into open water. As the dawn fog lifted, we saw the wallowing surf that waited for us. Some Kwakwaka'wakw elders at T'sakis had predicted a sea like glass. Others told us stories of lost seiners and sudden shifts of temper in the unpredictable sea we were going to cross. "If you don't know how to handle those waves, you won't make it," said one old fisherman cheerfully. "I've seen her change from easy to crazy in a few minutes."

A cedar canoe handles water differently from any other vessel. A kayak bobs on top of the waves, light as a leaf and leaving as little wake as a diving duck. A fishing boat digs through the swells, dragging nets as heavy as roots. Pleasure craft bounce on the chop, and large liners keep the traveller as far as possible from the wet, dark ocean. It is the canoe that participates in the sea, riding the waves and carving through the roll like a pilot whale. It is sometimes airborne, sometimes as stable as its aboriginal tree.

As we set out, our cedar canoe came off the whitecap of a wave and dropped into a well, from the top of the world to the bottom in one insistent glide. A well-made canoe can drop off a high swell over and over on a long journey like a cat leaping from a rock and receive no damage. A poorly worked canoe can slam down into a trough twenty or thirty times and then split like a weary argument, spilling its pullers irretrievably into the cold current.

Any fears of broken canoes faded in the spirit of our ride. We were moving in phalanx towards Clam Beach on Fury Island, the traditional gathering site of the Rivers Inlet Oweekeno people. The Jamestown S'Klallam canoe, with a ring of red woven cedar draped over the prow, bucked the swells determinedly. The song of its pullers seemed to sparkle like sunlight. The Campbell River, Weiwaikum and Fort Rupert T'Sakis canoes travelled as if returning to waters they remembered well.

I tried to keep track of the eleven other canoes around us. Soon it was impossible, as each canoe moved to meet the sea on its own terms. I gave up scanning the swells and concentrated on our work. I wondered how our fragile, humble craft could make any headway against the endless hills and gulleys of the sea. I wondered how long we could use our simple paddle rhythms and exhaustible bodies to stay with the limitless roll of waves heading for Asia. Then, suddenly, I found an energy that came from all directions, from the wind and my fellow pullers, from the water and the sun glancing off the cliffs of the distant shore. I was filled with the song that is known by those who go beyond themselves, and the name of that music is joy.

For a few days we were feasted at Clam Beach, beyond the reach of electricity. We camped along the shell-white beach and sang, ate herring eggs dried on kelp leaves and forged our community with drums and stories. One evening Maurice Nahanee and I crouched in the rain on rocks at the far end of the lagoon and listened to his Squamish crew drumming and singing around the campfire as night fell. By then we had been travelling so long we almost forgot whether we were damp or dry. Maurice gripped the paddle he had carved, with which he had been showing me a Squamish war dance, and smiled softly. "This is how things must have been on the old journeys."

The only things out of place were the nylon tent domes planted above the tide lines. "Our southern folks are beginning to sing your northern songs," I agreed. "That's how the feasts teach us to share."

My friend, who had adopted his Salish name of Gilk Buwx, stood to leave. "I think I'd better join my family," he said. I watched as he went to bring his voice to the circle of disciplined men and women. The Squamish crew had matching canoe uniforms and a group morale that shamed the rest of us. They had prepared for their journey by sweatbath cleansing, spirit bathing and traditional spiritual methods. From their tight circle they sang prayers to the Creator each morning before entering their canoes. When they danced, the lines of small carved paddles on their plum-red vests moved in unison. They taught the rest of us a great deal.

I stayed a while in the shadows, enjoying a vision of the ancient feasts the Oweekeno had called here, out of the Queen Charlotte storm path. Finally I was drawn across the narrow bridge of sand to where my canoe-mates sat drumming, remembering the words of the old songs, laughing at the old jokes, many nations singing until dawn.

All of our canoes travelled up the Inside Passage of Vancouver Island except that of the Makah. Against the wishes of the U.S. Coast Guard, they travelled on their ancient and accustomed route to their relatives on the west coast of the island. When they landed, coming in off savage seas and thirty-mile-an-hour winds, they were lifted, still in their canoe, and carried by the people of Nuu-chah-nulth into the bighouse. Makah pullers still speak today with pride of the honour of their return.

It was when we reached Bella Bella and met the thousands of people who had come that I finally understood how the Canoe Way of Knowledge informs all aspects of Northwest Coast life. This vessel of family connects us to spirit and the old world at the same time as it gives us hope for the future. Each nation made an extended presentation about who they were, with coppers displayed, new songs brought forward, challenges thrown out and feasts shared. At 4:00 A.M., when the last nation had gotten us up to dance, I felt the energy this great spirit canoe gave us all. The final barrier was broken, and it was time to go home together.

On the return pull from Bella Bella, we had a difficult time of it recrossing stormy Queen Charlotte Sound. The Elwha *Warrior* and the *International* waited out the storm at Clam Beach, this time without the crowds and feasting, and then made our bold run across the heavy chop. Porpoises rolled with us, as if assuring us that sea change wasn't so bad and that we could make it to shore by following their lead.

When we pulled into the bay of Fort Rupert and saw the Kwagiutl village of T'Sakis across from us in the afternoon calm, our relief went out in a great cheer. We hoisted our sails to catch the fresh wind and headed towards land, warm showers, hot food and a chance to rest a few days before our final plunge south. Our craft were now gliding, with no support boats behind us. Tom Jackson of La Push, respected and weathered leader of the Washington State Canoe Nation contingent and Shaker preacher, reached for his canoe bailer, smiling disarmingly at me.

"Hello, Tom," he said, his eyes alight as he scooped a cold slosh of salt water over me. "Hello, Tom," I responded, laughing and hitting him with a great splash from my paddle. Al Charles Jr. stopped steering long enough to get both of us with a great wave, and soon we were spraying each other with abandon, roaring with laughter. Banjo was heaving water with both hands on Conrad, who shook with the hilarity of it all and was unable to launch his own counterattack.

Our water fight continued as the wind drew us to shore. A T'Sakis elder waited for us there, his eyes glistening with tears. He watched us lower the sails, circle the harbour in ceremony and back onto the pebbly low-tide strand. Apparently he had missed our mock combat.

"Oh," he said, "I never thought I'd live to see this day again. Canoes coming in without those motorized modern boats behind you, sails up, proud and strong, just like in the old days." He lifted his hands to us as we dragged our canoes above the tide line. Then he came up and patted us on the back. "But why are you all so wet?" he said, puzzled. When we finally stopped laughing, we began to tell him the story of our return.

THE TEN RULES OF THE CANOE

*The Ten Rules of the Canoe were developed
by the Quileute canoe contingent for a Northwest Experiential Education
Conference in 1990.*

---

1. EVERY STROKE WE TAKE IS ONE LESS WE HAVE TO MAKE.

Keep going! Even against the most relentless wind or retrograde tide, somehow a canoe moves forward. This mystery can only be explained by the fact that each pull forward is real movement and not delusion.

2. THERE IS TO BE NO ABUSE OF SELF OR OTHERS.

Respect and trust cannot exist in anger. It has to be thrown overboard, so the sea can cleanse it. It has to be washed off the hands and cast into the air, so the stars can take care of it. We always look back at the shallows we pulled through, amazed at how powerful we thought those dangers were.

3. BE FLEXIBLE.

The adaptable animal survives. If you get tired, ship your paddle and rest. If you get hungry, put in on the beach and eat a few oysters. If you can't figure one way to make it, do something new. When the wind confronts you, sometimes you're supposed to go the other way.

4. THE GIFT OF EACH ENRICHES ALL.

Every story is important. The bow, the stern, the skipper, the power puller in the middle — everyone is part of the movement. The elder sits in her cedar at the front, singing her paddle song, praying for us all. The weary paddler resting is still ballast. And there is always that time when the crew needs some joke, some remark, some silence to keep going, and the least likely person provides.

5. WE ALL PULL AND SUPPORT EACH OTHER.

Nothing occurs in isolation. When we aren't in the family of a canoe, we are not ready for whatever comes. The family can argue, mock, ignore each other at its worst, but that family will never let itself sink. A canoe that lets itself sink is certainly wiser never to leave the beach. When we know that we are not alone in our actions, we also know we are lifted up by everyone else.

6. A HUNGRY PERSON HAS NO CHARITY.

Always nourish yourself. The bitter person, thinking that sacrifice means self-destruction, shares mostly anger. A paddler who doesn't eat at the feasts doesn't have enough strength to paddle in the morning. Take that sandwich they throw you at 2:00 A.M.! The gift of who you are only enters the world when you are strong enough to own it.

7. EXPERIENCES ARE NOT ENHANCED THROUGH CRITICISM.

Who we are, how we are, what we do, why we continue, flourish with tolerance. The canoe fellows who are grim go one way. The men and women who find the lightest flow may sometimes go slow, but when they arrive they can still sing. And they have gone all over the sea, into the air with the seagulls, under the curve of the wave with the dolphin and down to the whispering shells, under the continental shelf. Withdrawing the blame acknowledges how wonderful a part of it all every one of us really is.

8. THE JOURNEY IS WHAT WE ENJOY.

Although the start is exciting and the conclusion gratefully achieved, it is the long, steady process we remember. Being part of the journey requires great preparation; being done with a journey requires great awareness; being on the journey, we are much more than ourselves. We are part of the movement of life. We have a destination, and for once, our will is pure, our goal is to go on.

9. A GOOD TEACHER ALLOWS THE STUDENT TO LEARN.

We can berate each other, try to force each other to understand, or we can allow each paddler to gain their awareness through the ongoing journey. Nothing sustains us like that sense of potential that we can deal with things. Each paddler learns to deal with the person in front, the person behind, the water, the air, the energy, the blessing of the eagle.

10. WHEN GIVEN ANY CHOICE AT ALL, BE A WORKER BEE — MAKE HONEY!

SELECTED BIBLIOGRAPHY

Adney, Edwin Tappan and Howard I. Chapelle. *The Bark Canoes and Skin Boats of North America.* United States National Museum. Bulletin 230. Washington, D.C.: Smithsonian Institution, 1964.

Arima, Eugene Y. A *Report on a West Coast Whaling Canoe Reconstructed at Port Renfrew, B.C.* Ottawa: History and Archaeology 5, Parks Canada, 1975.

Boas, Franz. *Kwakiutl Ethnography.* Edited by Helen Codere. Chicago: University of Chicago Press, 1966.

Buerge, David. "Salt Water Itinerary." In "The Seasonal Round of Activity," a manuscript of the Duwamish, 1983.

Collison, William. *In the Wake of the War Canoe.* 1915. Reprint Victoria: Sono Nis Press, 1981.

Duff, Wilson. "Thoughts on the Nootka Canoe." In *The World Is as Sharp as a Knife: An Anthology in Honour of Wilson Duff.* Edited by Donald N. Abbott. Victoria: British Columbia Provincial Museum in association with Donors Fund, Friends of the Museum, 1981.

Durham, Bill. "Canoes from Cedar Logs: A Study of Early Types and Designs." *Pacific Northwest Quarterly* 46, no. 2 (1955): 33–39.

Gould, R. "Seagoing Canoes among the Indians of Northwestern California." *Ethnohistory* 15 (1964): 11–42.

Hamilton, Gordon. "War Canoe Races Still Excite Coast Indians." *Canadian Geographic* 2, no. 4 (1980): 38–45.

Holm, Bill. "Carving a Kwakiutl Canoe." *The Beaver* (summer 1961): 28–35.

Kennedy, Dorothy and Randy Bouchard. *Sliammon Life, Sliammon Lands.* Vancouver: Talonbooks, 1983.

Lincoln, Leslie. *Coast Salish Canoes.* Seattle: Center for Wooden Boats, 1991.

Millar, Kathryn. "Traditional Nuu-Chah-Nulth Canoes." Teachers' Resource Book, Alberni District Secondary School.

Neel, David. "Bella Bella: The Rebirth of the Northwest Coast Canoe." *Native Peoples* 7, no. 2 (1994): 10–18.

Neel, David. "The Rebirth of the Long-Distance Paddlers." *Beautiful British Columbia* 35 (winter 1993): 6–13.

Powell, Jay and Vickie Jensen. *Quileute: An Introduction to the Indians of La Push.* Seattle: University of Washington Press, 1976.

Quileute Tribal School. *Paddle to Seattle.* Edited by Mark Mascarin. 1990. 43 min. Videocassette.

Roberts, Kenneth G. and Philip Shackleton. *The Canoe: A History of the Craft from Panama to the Arctic.* Camden: International Marine Publishing Company, 1983.

Stewart, Hilary. *Cedar: Tree of Life to the Northwest Coast Indians.* Vancouver: Douglas and McIntyre, 1984.

———. *Indian Fishing: Early Methods on the Northwest Coast.* Vancouver: Douglas and McIntyre, 1977.

Suquamish Tribal Museum. *Waterborne: Gift of the Indian Canoe.* Seattle: Current-Rutledge, 1989. Audiovisual production.